CHRISTIAN FAITH AND
GREEK PHILOSOPHY

Christian Faith
and
Greek Philosophy

A. H. Armstrong
and
R. A. Markus

DARTON, LONGMAN & TODD
LONDON

DARTON, LONGMAN & TODD LTD
29a Gloucester Road
London, S.W.7

BR 128 . G8
A 75 1960

1) Philosophy, Ancient
2) Greece - Religion

CONTENTS

PREFACE

There have been few longer, or, perhaps, more fruitful dialogues in the history of human thought than that between Christianity and Greek philosophy. It began in the second century A.D. when persons with some tincture of philosophical culture began to enter the Church and philosophers who felt no temptation to do so began to scrutinize with superior indignation this impertinent barbarian apparition: and this first encounter had of course been preceded by a long period during which Hellenic philosophy had exercised some influence on the thought of Greek-speaking Jews. It is still going on today, wherever Christians or non-Christians consider the Christian faith with minds formed by the study of the Greek philosophers. 'Dialogue' is the only proper word for it. And by saying this we do not mean to give any undue importance to the polemic of Christians against pagans and pagans against Christians, to the Apologists and their many successors or to Celsus, Porphyry and Julian; like most ancient controversies, these set debates had too much prejudice in them, and too little understanding of the other side's position, to be really fruitful. We mean rather the dialogue which went on in the minds of Christians who came to the Bible and the teachings of the Church with minds already trained in and full of Greek philosophy, or turned to read the philosophers with minds already formed by Bible and Church, the tension and interplay of revealed doctrine and philosophical ideas. This was much more important than set external controversies, and played a much greater part in shaping Christian thought: and it is a sort of dialogue which goes on today, which can break out at any moment in the mind of any Christian who reads those obstinately vital and perennially disturbing or inspiring books, the works of Plato, Aristotle and Plotinus. Plato, for whom books were dead images of living conversation, which went on saying the same thing for ever, would have been surprised, and perhaps rather pleased, to find how many different things his books, and those of the great philosophers whom he taught or inspired, have said to successive generations from his time to our own, and how many vigorous discussions and fruitful trains of thought they have stimulated. And some Christians would find it equally surprising to discover how much in their own Christian language has its origins in the work of these pagan philosophers.

This book is an attempt to describe some particularly important episodes in the dialogue. It is concerned chiefly with its first phase, when pagan Greek philosophy still had an independent life not confined to books, and the tradition of Christian thought was still in the process of formation. It is not, however, confined to the period of the Fathers. On some topics one particular part of this great dialogue, the conversation with Aristotle, did not make its impact on Christianity until the thirteenth century. It would have been a serious distortion of the picture to ignore this altogether merely because it came later.

We are very conscious of the amount that this book leaves out. There is, for instance, no proper discussion of the problem of evil as it appeared to Greek and Christian thinkers: and we have made no attempt even to indicate how the dialogue went when it got on to political topics.

About this last subject we felt that very many current presentations of the differences between Christian and pagan thought were over-simplified and unsatisfactory, but that the real situation was so complex that any attempt to disentangle it and give even an approximately true account, one in particular which did justice to the remarkable variety of Christian political thinking, would carry us far beyond the necessary limits of this book, and probably beyond our own capacities. And on the whole, in so vast a field where severe selection is necessary, we have thought it best to confine ourselves to topics in which we are really interested and about which we think we have something to say which may interest others.

The book is based on lectures originally delivered under the auspices of the Extra-Mural Department of the University of Liverpool. Chs. 1–5 are by A. H. Armstrong, 6–10 by R. A. Markus. Although we are each responsible for our own chapters, we have discussed them with each other very thoroughly, so that this book itself is the product of a dialogue, and may perhaps seem to its readers, as it seems to us, to have the sort of unity, combined with differences of emphasis and interpretation, which one might expect to find in a real conversation, of a friendly and constructive sort, on a subject of such importance and complexity.

We wish to thank the Editor of the *Downside Review* for permission to reprint some passages which have already appeared in print in that periodical (especially large portions of Chs. 4 and 7). We are both very grateful indeed to Mrs. M. C. Markus for her work on the typescript and for preparing the Index.

I

God and the World Creation

THE first Greeks who told stories about the beginnings of things generally thought of the world as born, rather than made. The history of the universe was for them a sort of family history, going back to an ultimate ancestor (Chaos in Hesiod, Night or Oceanus in other early accounts). The gods are part of the family, *in* the world, not its outside causes or makers. Heaven and Earth themselves are great gods as well as natural regions, the ancestors of the other gods as well as the origins of all other things. The teller of stories about the origin of the gods called Pherecydes of Syros, who lived in the sixth century B.C. and may possibly have been influenced by the earliest Greek philosophy, does seem to speak, in an odd and allegorical way, of Zeus making at least the world we know; for he describes him making a great tapestry or embroidered cloth with Earth and Ocean on it as a wedding-present for his bride Chthonie—perhaps the Earth-principle, or basic earth, the substructure as distinct from the variegated surface. But Pherecydes also elsewhere used the language of generation rather than making, when he represented the primal stuff as being the seed of Chronos, his third everlasting first being, along with Zas (Zeus) and Chthonie: and in any case Zeus's weaving is not an act of creation out of nothing in the Christian sense but a working on pre-existing material. As such it is an interesting anticipation of the ordering of the world by a divine intelligence conceived by later Greek philosophers: but among the early storytellers Pherecydes' idea of divine craftsmanship is, as far as we know, an isolated exception to the generative way of thinking.

The earliest Greek philosophers, the Milesians, follow the generative pattern of mythical thinking, with one important development; they seem to have thought explicitly of their first principles as everlasting (as Pherecydes did, perhaps under their influence). Hesiod, on the other hand, was content to say that his Chaos 'came into being', without explaining why, how, or from what; that is, Chaos seems to be for him not an everlasting principle but simply the first ancestor, beyond whom the genealogy cannot be traced back any further. The idea of a world-directing intelligence appears at the end of the sixth century, with Xenophanes and Heraclitus (Anaximander the Milesian may possibly have believed in an elementary sort of cosmic law and order). In the system of the fifth century philosopher Anaxagoras intelligence not only directs but forms the world from pre-existing matter: and from this and other fifth century doctrines Plato developed the idea, which is central to his philosophical religion, of a divine intelligence which forms and rules the world, ordering everything for the best. This divine intelligence is symbolized by the great Craftsman, the Demiurge, of the *Timaeus*, a dialogue which perhaps had more influence on early Christian thought than any other single Greek philosophical writing. We should note that what is symbolically expounded in the *Timaeus* (and more plainly stated in other dialogues) is not the Jewish-Christian doctrine of creation, though Jews and

Christians read their own beliefs into Plato. The Craftsman is not certainly the supreme or only divine principle, and he is limited by the imperfections of an eternally existing irrationality in things, a disorderly motion produced by a 'vagabond principle', for whose existence he does not appear to be responsible. A feature of Plato's theology which is of importance in considering the influence of Greek philosophy on Christian thinking is his deeply-held conviction that the divine power orders everything for the best, and can be shown to do so; that God not only has a good and wise purpose in everything he does, but a purpose which the wise man can discern and explain convincingly to the foolish unbeliever. This idea appears first in Greek thought in the fifth century, in the philosophy of Diogenes of Apollonia. Plato probably inherited it from his master Socrates. The Stoics adopted it with uncritical enthusiasm, and the Christians took it over, with a collection of stock arguments and examples, from the Platonists and Stoics. In this way there began that long series of attempts to explain and justify the ways of God in creation and history, to show an obvious goodness and rationality in his arrangement of the heavenly bodies, his provision for the nourishment of lions or intestinal parasites, his dealings with societies or individuals, which have seldom proved convincing and are sometimes quite embarrassingly silly and unpleasant. A conviction that God does in some way order everything for the best seems to be an essential part of belief in him, if we mean by God what Christians have always meant. But it is quite compatible with a belief that his purposes are mysterious and hard or impossible to discover when he has not revealed them; a belief often enough expressed in the Bible, best of all in that great protest against a too facile theodicy, the Book of Job.

But though Plato did not agree quite as closely with the Christians and was not quite as helpful to them as they thought, he and his followers had more to offer them than any school of later origin. In Aristotle the universe depends on the divine only because the divine is, in Aristotle's own language its 'final cause'; the universe and everything in it aspires consciously or unconsciously to imitate the divine perfection, which is a self-enclosed thinking about its own thinking without knowledge of or concern for the universe, and this aspiration is the driving force which keeps the heavenly spheres in everlasting rotation, and is ultimately responsible for all movement and change, all coming-to-be and passing-away in a world which is eternal as a whole, without beginning or end. The Stoic God certainly generates (out of his own substance) and orders the universe in every detail, but he does so as a material immanent force, a sort of perfectly good and wise gas. None the less, many Stoics treated their curious deity as a personal God to whom they felt a real and deep devotion; and the Christians, even when they remained unaffected by Stoic materialism,[1] found Stoic religion edifying and took from the Stoics many of their arguments from Providence and the divine ordering of the world.

But it was the later Platonism of the Christian era, which interpreted Plato and developed his teaching with the help of ideas derived from Aristotle and the Stoics, which the Christians found closest to their own ideas. In this Platonism the making and direction of the world by either the supreme, or, more usually, a second divine intelligence was emphasized; and its doctrine that the Platonic Ideas or Forms exist in the mind of God (which goes back at least to the first

[1]Some were affected by it, notably Tertullian and the Monarchians (on the latter see below, Ch. 3).

century B.C.) removed the obscurity present in Plato about the relationship of the craftsman-divinity to his model. This doctrine, and the conception of the 'Second Mind' or 'Second God', will be discussed more fully in Ch. 3, 'The Word and the Ideas'. Finally, in the greatest of the late Platonic philosophers, Plotinus (third century A.D.), there appears for the first time clearly and unmistakably in Greek thought the doctrine of a transcendent Source of Being from which all things derive their existence, which is cause of being and not only of world-formation and world-order. This doctrine of the total dependence of all things for their existence on the One or Good, which has its origin in a famous and mysterious passage of Plato's *Republic*,[1] though it is not identical with the Christian doctrine of creation, probably influenced (directly or indirectly) its later philosophical formulation by patristic and mediaeval thinkers. But Christian thought about creation did not derive from Platonism or any other Greek philosophy. It started from the simple affirmation of Genesis I.i. 'In the beginning God made heaven and earth', which the Christians following Jewish tradition,[2] interpreted as implying creation 'out of nothing', i.e. without any eternally existing material which did not owe its being to God. For the earlier Christian thinkers the idea that all things were wholly dependent on God for their existence was inseparably bound up with the idea of a beginning of time in which the world was created. The question of the eternity of the world became one of the principal points of controversy between Christians and pagan philosophers; other doctrines of late Greek philosophy which will be touched on

[1] VI. 509 B.
[2] The first explicit statement that God created the world out of nothing is II Maccabees, 7.28 (date after 125 B.C.).

in Chs. 3 and 4 helped to give it importance, the ideas of the universe as a necessary expression of the supreme divinity and as itself divine in a subordinate degree, and therefore everlasting, and containing lesser everlasting visible deities, the beings of the Upper Cosmos, the heavenly bodies. St. Thomas Aquinas, following and developing a distinction made by St. Augustine, clearly separated the two ideas of total dependence and of a beginning of the created world[1]: he held that the truth of the first could be philosophically demonstrated, but that of the second could not, any more than that of its contrary; as a Catholic Christian he believed it as an article of faith, but did not think that the question could be settled philosophically.

Christian thinkers, then, did not derive their idea of creation from Greek philosophy (though they often read it into the Greek philosophers, particularly into Plato's *Timaeus*). They did however take from them ideas and arguments which played an important part in the philosophical formulation of their own doctrine; the ideas of a First Cause and of a Source of Being (the former, inevitably and always, in a Platonic rather than an Aristotelian form, in spite of Aquinas's use of drastically revised and adapted Aristotelian arguments to demonstrate its existence, since God, the Christian First Cause, must know and intend his effects); and the arguments for the existence of a good and wise Creator, especially the much used argument from design. Perhaps one of the points at which Greek philosophical influence on Christian thinking about creation is most apparent is to be found in the readiness of Christian thinkers to see evidence of the Creator in the order and regularity of the physical universe, in the unchanging

[1] cp. *Summa Theologiae* I. 46.2. *Contra Gentes* II. 31–38. St. Augustine *City of God* X. 31. XI. 4.

operation of its laws. The idea of creation as an expression of God's eternal wisdom ordaining laws and bounds for all things is certainly found in the Jewish Scriptures (apart from the Wisdom-literature written under some degree of Greek influence), notably in the Psalms. Nor was the idea of 'special providences' and extraordinary divine interventions by any means alien to the Greek religious mind. But it does seem to be true that the Greek philosophers (in distinction from the ordinary religious Greek) saw evidence of divine existence and action almost exclusively in the order and regularity of nature, and that the Jews, even more than religious men elsewhere, saw God's power and wisdom manifested particularly in unique and extraordinary events, interruptions of the normal course of things. So on the whole it appears to be fair to say that when Christian thinkers lay stress on the ordered succession and reliability of natural processes as pointing back to God the designer and ruler of the universe they are influenced by Greek philosophy, directly or indirectly, though they are saying nothing inconsistent with the Bible. Catholic theology, from the Fathers to our own day, has always tried to keep a balance between the two emphases, not denying or under-valuing extraordinary divine interventions, but always see-ing them against a background of natural law and order in which God's power and wisdom are continually evident.

2

God's Transcendence and Infinity

BY God's transcendence one of two things can be meant, both in their way attempts to express his overwhelming superiority to all else. The first is that he is *remote*, only accessible through a hierarchy of inferior divine beings or powers, or, in the most simple-minded form of the doctrine, actually outside and above the world. This way of thinking about God's transcendence was common in late Greek philosophy, and has sometimes affected Christian theology. The idea that God lives on the top of the outermost sphere of heaven appears in the treatise *On the Universe*,[1] falsely attributed to Aristotle, and it, or something like it, has always been common among simple-minded Christians, though it is certainly not orthodox Christian doctrine. But the other meaning of transcendence is much more important for serious Christian thinking. This is that God is *wholly other*, different from and better than everything that we are or can know. This kind of transcendence is compatible with the deepest immanence; the two are in fact different ways of looking at the same thing. Just because

[1] *De Mundo* Ch. 6. 397 B ff. The date of this treatise is probably late first century B.C., perhaps somewhat later. It is one of the most important documents of the 'cosmic religion' (on which see Ch. 4).

God is other than all things he is free from the sundering limitations of every definite thing and can be immediately present to all things everywhere. Not only is he not in space or time at all, he is free from all other boundaries and limitations. This kind of doctrine of divine transcendence is at least hinted at in Plato: it begins to appear in the later Platonic philosophy of the first centuries A.D. In the short summary of Platonic teaching produced by the second century Platonist Albinus we find its characteristic form of expression, the 'negative theology', in which every statement we can make about God is denied as inadequate.[1] This reaches its fullest development and finest expression in Plotinus's doctrine of the One or Good, the transcendent source of being who is himself beyond being and thought, whom our thought and language cannot describe or encompass but only point to and reach towards without ever attaining. This kind of doctrine of transcendence expressed in negative terms was accepted by Christians, as soon as they began to think philosophically, as expressing their conviction of the mystery and majesty of God.[2] Already before Plotinus at the end of the second century A.D., it appears in the thought of Clement of Alexandria,[3] and it

---

[1] Albinus, *Epitome*, Ch. 10. 'God is not genus or species . . . qualified or unqualified . . . part or like a whole having parts. The first way of thinking about him is by taking away all these things . . . the second by analogy.'

[2] They could not, of course, and did not want to deny that the positive language of Scripture was a proper way, and the best possible human way, of speaking about God, but insisted that like all human language it was symbolic or analogical and that in using it we must purge our minds of the human imperfections and limitations it suggests and see it as pointing to an inconceivable reality.

[3] cp. E. F. Osborn *The Philosophy of Clement of Alexandria* (Cambridge, 1957), Ch. 2.

appears earlier still in the Gnostics.[1] It has been accepted, and the language of negative (in Eastern Christian terminology 'apophatic') theology used ever since, not only by the great mystics to express the ineffability of their own experience, but by sober and balanced Christian philosophers like Aquinas as a necessary element in any truthful human speaking about God.

There is however one interesting difference between the Greek philosophical and the Christian use of this language of transcendence. The Greeks are very shy of attributing infinity to God, though it seems to us naturally and necessarily implied by this way of thinking. The Christians, in this following Philo the Jew of Alexandria, speak of God as infinite without any hesitation or qualification. When, however, we come to appreciate the historical and linguistic reasons for the Greek reluctance to speak of God as infinite, we can see that perhaps the difference in thought at this point between Greeks and Christians does not go as deep as might be supposed. This is particularly true in the case of Plotinus, the one great Greek philosopher who does, with many hesitations and qualifications, come to speak of God as in some sense infinite. It is worth while to examine his thought about God's infinity and its background in order to understand better the differences and the points of contact between late Greek and contemporary Christian thought.

The idea of an unbounded, unlimited, indefinite element in the nature of things goes back to the very beginnings of Greek philosophy. Already in Anaximander (sixth century B.C.) we meet the *apeiron*, the unbounded, inexhaustible reservoir of living stuff from which all things come and to

[1]cp. Basileides in Hippolytus *Refutation of all Heresies* VII. 21. (Stevenson, *A New Eusebius* No. 52).

which they return: and in the Pythagorean-Platonic tradition the Unlimited is the inseparable correlative of Limit,
the formless substrate from which formed, definite things
come to be by the imposition of Form. In the later thought
of Plato a formless, indefinite element, the Great-and-Small
or Indefinite Dyad, appears as one of the ultimate constituents of the World of Forms itself. But the idea that the
first principle of things, the supreme divinity, is itself in
some sense infinite, does not seem to appear clearly and
unmistakably in the Greek-speaking world before Philo of
Alexandria. In the normal Greek, and especially in the
Platonic-Pythagorean, way of thinking the good and the
divine is essentially form and definition, light and clarity, as
opposed to vague formless darkness. The Greek philosophical vocabulary has no word for 'infinite' which does
not convey the idea of vague formless indefiniteness; to say
that God is *apeiros* or *aoristos* would normally to a Greek
philosopher imply not only that he was free from all limit
or determination but that he was a vague dim sort of something which was nothing in particular. It is hard enough
for a Christian philosopher to explain why God's infinity
does not imply indefinite vagueness; for a Greek philosopher
it was very much more difficult. This should be borne in
mind when considering the thought of Plotinus, who was
the first in the authentic Greek philosophical tradition to
try to work out with any sort of precision the senses in which
infinity can be predicated of the Godhead and to distinguish
them from the evil infinity of matter, which is formlessness
and indefinite multiplicity. How serious and urgent the
problem of separating the two infinities was for him we
can understand from the first words of his treatise *On
Numbers*,[1] 'Is multiplicity a falling away from the One, and

[1] VI 6 [34].

unboundedness a complete falling away because it is an uncountable multiplicity, and is unboundedness therefore evil, and are we evil when we are a multiplicity?' Plotinus's thought about divine infinity can be summarized as follows.[1] *Apeiros* for Plotinus means simply 'in some sense without limit (*peras*)', and when he applies it to divine being he does so most often to the inferior divine hypostases, Intellect and Soul, and in a relative, not an absolute sense; he regards them that is, as realities which are unbounded in one way but limited in another. Thus they are infinite in power in the sense that their power is inexhaustible; it pervades everything and you can never come to the end of it. Or they are infinite, or rather unbounded, in the sense that they have the complete and simultaneous unity proper to eternal non-spatial spiritual being, in which there is absence of limit by division in the sense that one part is not *here* and another *there*, one does not exist *now* and another *then*. Or Divine Intellect is infinite, without limit because it is all-inclusive and so unincluded, immeasurable as having nothing outside to measure it and as being itself the absolute standard of measurement. This idea of 'unmeasured measure' is applied by Plotinus to the One;[2] but it is worth noting that when he speaks of the First Principle in this way he does not use the term 'unbounded'. In fact, though in the thought of Plotinus only the One or Good is infinite in the absolute sense in which we speak of the infinity of God, he is reluctant to speak of him as *apeiros* or *aoristos*; this is a reluctance which is easy to understand in view of what has

[1] For detailed discussion see my article 'Plotinus's Doctrine of the Infinite and Christian Thought' in *Downside Review*, Winter, 1954–55, pp. 47–58: cp. also the discussion between L. Sweeney and W. N. Clark, *Gregorianum* 38 (1957), pp. 515–35; 713–32: 40 (1959), pp. 75–98; 327–31.

[2] V 5 [32] 4.

been said about the history and implications of the terms. He will say that the power of the One is unbounded, or that he is the source of infinity; but he prefers to express the infinity of the One in terms of the 'negative theology', by denying that any of our names or concepts (including 'One' and 'Good'), which necessarily involve the thought of some kind of limitation, can strictly be applied to him; and in particular by refusing to apply to him the predicate of existence. For in the thought of Plotinus being and essence or form (*on* and *ousia*) are inseparable correlatives; 'being' means always 'being this or that', particular, defined, limited being, and that which is beyond form is necessarily beyond being.[1] So that when he says that the One 'does not exist' he is simply denying that he is in any way limited in the strongest possible terms.

For Plotinus the One was certainly incomprehensible, and was so because of his absence of limitation. But the Christian writers, because they have no hesitation in speaking of God as *apeiros*, can bring out more clearly than Plotinus the close relationship between his infinity and his incomprehensibility. In their thought and language the two are very closely and frequently conjoined. St. John Chrysostom, for instance, in his sermons *On the Incomprehensibility of God*, brings out the connexion very clearly.[2] There is also another interesting and important difference between the language used by the Christians about God's infinity and incomprehensibility and that used by Plotinus. The Christian Fathers never allow us to forget that they are speaking of an infinite and incomprehensible person, however much his infinite personality may transcend the limited personalities of our experience; for they are always

[1] V 5 [32] 6.
[2] cp. especially I. 705B, 706B.

speaking of God as he is revealed in the Scriptures. Plotinus too thinks of the One or Good as a personal God in the sense that he attributes to him something analogous to what we know as intellect and will in a manner proper to his transcendent unity. But he often and quite naturally falls into an impersonal way of speaking about him, especially when he is considering the relationship to him of the beings which derive their existence from him. It would be an entirely misleading generalization to say that the Greek philosophical conception of God is impersonal; rather, there is a continual tension and interplay between personal and impersonal ways of thinking about God, between thinking about him in terms of human thought and action and thinking about him in terms of natural forces or abstract concepts, which appears as crude, if rather likeable, inconsistency in the Stoics, but is also present in subtler forms in the thought of Plato and Aristotle.

The close connexion between the infinity and the incomprehensibility of God in the thought of the Christian Fathers indicates the lasting service which the 'negative theology' has to render to Christian thinking. This is to remind us that when we speak of God as Infinite Being, Infinite Goodness, and so on, the prefixed 'Infinite' is not just an empty compliment to his Divine Majesty. It is to remind us that we are speaking of that which utterly transcends our words and thoughts. Christian philosophers and theologians (especially those of the scholastic tradition) are sometimes perhaps too much inclined to try to catch God in their net of concepts, to think that they can express him well enough for all practical purposes in a tidily arranged set of clear and distinct ideas. So it is good that we should sometimes confront ourselves with even Plotinus's most extreme negations, his statements that the One 'does not think' or 'does not exist', and should realize that they have a genuine and important meaning, that the mystery before which the angels veil their faces shatters our concepts of being and thought and cannot be contained within them. It is desperately important that we should maintain, however difficult the assertion may be to justify, that we can distinguish between truth and falsehood, sense and non-sense, in our statements about God. But we must not formulate our assertion about the way in which we can make true and meaningful statements about God so that it deceives ourselves or other people into thinking that we can comprehend him or are justified in pushing his incomprehensibility into the back of our minds and never adverting to it in practice.

3

The Word and the Ideas

THE most characteristic feature of Plato's philosophy, for
most of his readers at any rate, is his doctrine that there
exist perfect, universal, eternal realities, the Forms or Ideas,
which are the objects of true knowledge and the standards
according to which we make judgements of value; the
objects which we encounter in the world of sense-experience
derive such reality and value as they have from some kind
of 'participation', never precisely defined, in these Forms,
or are imitations of them made by a divine intelligent
power. As we have seen in Ch. 1, the later Platonism of the
Christian era (which both Christians and pagans accepted
as a true interpretation of Plato's thought) placed these
archetypes in a Divine Mind, either the mind of the Maker
of the world or of a supreme intelligence which the Demiurge contemplates and from which he derives the pattern
of the world-order he causes. The form of the doctrine in
which the Ideas are the plan in the mind of the Maker, the
Divine Architect's complete and detailed conception of the
universe he constructs, goes back at least to the first century
B.C. It appears in Philo (30 B.C.–after A.D. 40), the Alexandrian Jew who uses Greek philosophy to interpret the
Jewish Scriptures. A later form of the doctrine, which makes

its first appearance, as far as our evidence goes, in the thought of the Middle Platonist Albinus in the second century A.D. makes the Ideas, placed in a divine mind higher than that which forms the world, not so much the 'architect's plan' (though they remain his model and source) as the all-inclusive richness of God's own spiritual and intellectual substance which is the object of his eternal self-contemplation. This is the result of a synthesis of the Platonic doctrine of the Ideas in the divine mind with Aristotle's doctrine that the divine mind 'thinks about its thinking', eternally contemplates itself because no other object is adequate to it.[1] Finally in Plotinus this self-contemplating divine mind which is the Ideas, which is the source of the soul which makes the world and of the formative principles for its making, itself proceeds from the One, the transcendent source of being which is beyond form or thought. Here we have the clearest example of the hierarchic subordination, the idea of a series of levels of divine and eternal being descending in order from the first principle, which occurs again and again in Greek thought of the later period. It is important to notice for our present purposes that this idea involves the fundamental axiom always assumed by late Greek philosophers that the product is always inferior to the producer.

In Philo of Alexandria, the Jewish thinker already referred to, the doctrine of the Ideas in the mind of God encounters an idea which appears in Jewish thought in the Wisdom-books of the Old Testament, reaching its fullest development in the Alexandrian Wisdom of Solomon (written by a Greek-speaking Jew some time before Philo,

[1]On this development see my paper 'The background of the Doctrine that the Intelligibles are not outside the Intellect' in *Entretiens Hardt* V (Vandoeuvres, Genève, 1960).

perhaps in the first half of the second century B.C.). This is the representation of the Wisdom of God as not merely an attribute but as a mysterious entity in some degree distinct from God, personal or quasi-personal (the poetic language of the Wisdom-books makes it difficult to determine how far in the thought of their authors Wisdom was really distinct or really personal), who was there 'in the beginning' with God, his companion and helper in creation. Jewish thought round about the Christian era was full of speculations about mysterious beings who were with the One God and through whom He created the world and revealed himself; in particular, in the thought of those Jewish religious groups in Palestine whom the orthodox Rabbis considered heretical, about whom we are now beginning to know a good deal, there is a great deal of speculation about 'Powers', about the 'Name of God', and about a mighty and mysterious being through whom God reveals himself, Jaoel or Metatron, the Angel of the Name.[1] Philo seems to have been influenced by this way of thinking in the form which it took among the Greek-speaking Jews of Alexandria, and to have combined it with the Platonic doctrine, and the idea which he probably took from the pseudo-Aristotelian treatise *On the Universe* (referred to in Ch. II) that God works through his powers, to produce his own distinctive theology. In this God works and manifests himself through Powers and a *Logos*, and in the *Logos* are the Platonic Ideas, the archetypes of all created things, the 'architect's plan' of creation. This is the first appearance of the word *Logos* in Jewish or Christian theology. It is a word in Greek of many meanings: among the chief are, reckoning, proportion, relation, explanation, argument, reason (in many senses), story, lan-

[1]On this heterodox Jewish thought and its influence see G. Quispel in *The Jung Codex* (London, 1955), pp. 61–78.

guage, grammatical sentence, and, in philosophical Greek from Aristotle onwards, formative principle. The Stoics used it of their God as the fiery rational forming principle of the universe, a use which they derived from the Pre-Socratic philosopher Heraclitus; they also used it for the formative principles of particular things, which are parts of God. In Neoplatonic philosophical language, from Plotinus onwards, *Logos* comes to mean frequently 'a power which represents or expresses a higher principle on a lower plane of being' a usage which may possibly be connected with Philo's employment of *Logos* for the instrumental creative and revealing principle.

When St. John calls Christ the *Logos* in the prologue of his Gospel it is not necessary to suppose that he had been reading Philo—as we have noticed already, speculations of this sort were widespread in Jewish circles round about the Christian era. When he uses this term all St. John can safely be assumed to be saying, from a scholar's point of view (theologians, using their own proper principles and methods, may rightly wish to go further), is that Christ's relationship to the Father is that of the Principle through whom the Father created the world and has now revealed himself in the world. But St. John's *Logos* is no longer a hazy and indefinite quasi-person or personification. He is undoubtedly a person, with a personal relationship to the Father—for he is Jesus Christ the Son. Another New Testament passage where the language of this kind of Jewish speculation is applied to the Son of God is the third verse of the first chapter of the Epistle to the Hebrews, where he is called *apaugasma tes doxes*, 'the outshining of his glory', a clear echo of Wisdom 7.23 *apaugasma phōtos aïdiou*, 'the outshining of everlasting light'.

When Christians began to develop a philosophical

theology in the second and third centuries A.D. it was
inevitable that they should, at first especially, be influenced
by, and express themselves in terms of, the characteristic
philosophy of the period; the penetration of contemporary
philosophical ideas into Christian thought was helped by
the sacred authority of the name *Logos*, with its Greek
philosophical associations and its important place in the
thought of Philo, whose influence on early Christian
thought, in particular on the Alexandrians Clement and
Origen, was, naturally, considerable. Now a distinctive
feature of the Platonism of the second and third centuries
A.D. (and of later pagan Neoplatonism) is the idea of a
hierarchy of divinities. At first (e.g. in Albinus) there are
two, the contemplative, transcendent divine mind and the
active divine mind which forms and rules the universe.
Later (in Numenius and Plotinus) there are three; in
Plotinus there is the transcendent One, the source of being,
from which proceeds the first mind, the contemplative one-
in-many in which the Platonic Forms are living thought,
and the third (as also in Numenius) is the intelligent soul
of the universe. This conception of the divine hierarchy
should be distinguished from the earlier, more simple-
minded view which saw God working on the universe
through his powers like a great Oriental monarch who does
everything through subordinates and intermediaries because he is too grand to do anything in person. The later
conception, where the emphasis is on the distinction between the active and contemplative divine minds, seems to
be the result of a purely Greek philosophical development,[1]

[1]This is not to say that particular philosophers were not influenced by Near Eastern speculation of Gnostic type. There is
some evidence that Numenius, especially, was so influenced (cp.
E. R. Dodds in *Entretiens Hardt*, V, "Numenius and Ammonius".)

which attempted to combine the purely contemplative God of Aristotle's *Metaphysics* with the active God of Plato's *Timaeus*.

Some of the first Christian theologians tended to subordinate the *Logos* to the Father, and sometimes the Holy Spirit to the Logos, very much as the pagan Platonists subordinated their principles to each other. They arranged the persons of the Trinity in descending order like the gods of Middle and Neoplatonism. The degree to which they did this depended on their closeness to the Greek philosophical tradition. Origen, who is the closest (he was probably a pupil of Plotinus's own master Ammonius Saccas), has a theology strikingly like that of Plotinus; the Father corresponds to the transcendent One; the Logos-Son, whom Origen makes much inferior to the Father, is the One-in-Many, the Divine Mind; the Spirit is inferior again, though not very like Plotinus's universal Soul. The New Testament's statements about the Holy Spirit made it difficult for even the most Platonically-minded theologian to assimilate him as completely to the Platonic World-Soul as the Son was assimilated to the Divine Mind. Later, Arianism shows signs of the influences of fourth-century Neoplatonism. The thought of the leading Arian theologian Eunomius, in particular, has affinities with that of contemporary Neoplatonists.[1] This kind of Subordinationist thinking produced a strong reaction to the opposite extreme from the end of the second century to the fourth. This was Monarchianism, which denied any real distinction between the divine Persons and saw them as phases in a single divine life, expanding into the world and withdrawing again into itself. Monarchianism was, at least as much as Subordinationism,

[1]cp. J. Daniélou 'Eunome l'Arien et l'Exegèse du Cratyle' in *Revue des Études Grecques*. T. 69. No. 326–8 (1956), pp. 412–32.

influenced by Greek philosophy, but the philosophy was not Platonism but Stoicism, with its doctrine of an expanding and contracting God who periodically produces the universe out of his substance and re-absorbs it into himself (see Ch. I).

Neither of these ways of thinking about the Trinity in terms of contemporary philosophy was approved by the Church. The solution of the problems raised in the discussions of the first centuries which was approved was that of St. Athanasius and Nicaea. We can only discuss it here from the point of view which concerns us, that of its relationship to late Greek philosophy. From this standpoint two things about it are especially notable; one is the denial of the pagan assumption that there can be degrees of divinity, that it is possibly to be more or less God; an assumption natural to a Greek philosopher, accustomed to use the word *theos* in a very wide and loose sense and to draw no very hard and fast line between the divinity and what came from it, but untenable by any adherent of the Jewish-Christian tradition, who, even if he spoke Greek, would use *Theos* in the exclusive sense of Jewish monotheism and always draw the clearest line between the Creator and his creation (extreme Subordinationist Christian thinkers always make that distinction far sharper than it is, for instance, in Plotinus; they slip into the Greek way of thinking when discussing the relationship of the Persons of the Trinity, but they never make an unbroken line of descent in decreasing degrees of divinity from the Father to the visible universe). The other is the denial of the basic (and quite arbitrary) assumption of late Greek hierarchic thinking that the product is always inferior to the producer. The Church in the Councils of Nicaea and Constantinople was able to free Christian teaching from the distortions introduced into it by these philosophical assumptions and the Stoic-inspired extreme reaction from their theological consequences, and to state that doctrine of the co-equal Trinity which she has maintained ever since, and which has been accepted by the vast majority of Christians as expressing the true sense of the New Testament and the earliest Christian tradition. In this doctrine the *Logos* is still seen as entirely originated from the Father. The Father is the *arche*, the absolute beginning, the principle and source of the divine life. The *Logos* is the Word of the Father, his self-expression. But he is a perfect, complete, infinitely adequate expression, and so *equal* to the Father, not inferior. And it then becomes easy to see the Spirit as a further co-equal expression of the Father and the Son's union in love, as their love itself, their delight and glory in each other.[1] And because Father, Son, and Spirit are all equal by being all fully God, each being the whole of the substance of the Godhead which is indivisible because infinite, they are Three Persons in One God.

The Trinity, so envisaged, becomes for the Christians what the divine cosmos was for the Greeks, the perfect self-expression of divinity. The Christian theologians insist as much as the Greeks that God in his perfection cannot be sterile and unproductive. If the Arians were right, says St. Athanasius, in their assertion that there was a time when the Son did not exist, then 'the Light was once without its

[1]This way of trying to state the mystery has not been adopted out of any desire to smuggle into the text an assertion that the *Filioque*, the doctrine that the Holy Spirit proceeds from the Father *and the Son*, was part of the creed of Nicaea (a Catholic would say that it was a necessary completion if the traditional faith was to be fully expressed). But as a Western Catholic the present writer finds himself quite incapable of stating the doctrine of the Trinity in any way satisfactory to himself which does not imply the *Filioque*.

shining and the Source was sterile and dry'.[1] But for the Christians the outpouring of divine productivity, the self-giving of divine love, reaches its unbounded term, its infinite fulfilment, within the Trinity. The created universe then appears as an 'extra', a magnificent and purely super-fluous expression of pure disinterested generosity, in the image and for the glory of the eternal *Logos*: and not, as it was for the pagan Platonists, the descending stages of divine self-expression, all necessary (in the sense that without them the Divine would be incomplete) and therefore all eternal (for to them even the visible universe was eternal as a whole). It may be argued, very reasonably, that if we try to think of God as not creating, to conceive him without this magnificent superfluity of giving, this extra generosity of creation, we must so diminish our thought of him that we are no longer really thinking about God at all: our thought about him will have become inadequate in a way in which it should not be, and not only in the way in which it must necessarily be. But it none the less remains true that we must attribute to him a freedom in creating of a kind which will prevent any confusion be-tween his creative act and the divine processions of Son and Holy Spirit and exclude any suggestion that creation is a necessary expansion or prolongation of procession.

With the clear statement of the doctrine of the co-equal Trinity in the fourth century the conception of the Ideas in the *Logos* forming an intermediate spiritual world inferior to the source of being, the Father, was abandoned. There was never any question of abandoning the doctrine of the Ideas in the mind of God, which has always remained an essential part of traditional Christian thinking. Nor was the close and special connexion of Ideas and Logos broken with

[1] *Against the Arians, Oration* I. 14.

the abandonment of hierarchic subordination. The Ideas were certainly from now onwards thought of, like all else in the Godhead, as the common property of the Trinity. But because the *Logos* is God's self-expression and creation is in his image, it has remained the tradition of Christian theology to associate the Ideas particularly with him. The doctrine of the Ideas in the mind of God underwent a long development in post-Nicene Christian thought, reaching its highest point of subtlety and elaboration in the thought of the great mediaeval scholastics, St. Bonaventure and St. Thomas, who agree to a remarkable extent in the details of their explanation of the doctrine, though they differ in their emphasis: in St. Bonaventure the stress is on the ideas as God's 'expression', the manifestation of his eternal productivity, and they are very closely connected therefore with the generation of the eternal Word. In St. Thomas the emphasis is on God's self-knowledge, of himself as eternally imitable in creation in an infinity of different ways. The two ways of looking at the doctrine are not of course incompatible, and both have their origins, as we have seen in late Platonic thought.[1] But the great problem which the scholastic expounders of the doctrine had to solve, that of reconciling the multiplicity of the Ideas with God's absolute unity was one which did not arise for the pagan Neoplatonists because of their sharp separation of the One from the One-in-Many, the divine mind containing the Ideas. This problem they solve by seeing all the Ideas as one thing, the single and simple divine essence known by God in a single and simple eternal regard which is the divine

[1] On these differing emphases, and on the whole scholastic doctrine of the Ideas, see Gilson's admirable chapter in his *Philosophy of St. Bonaventure*, tr. Illtyd Trethowan and F. J. Sheed (London, 1940), pp. 139–61.

essence itself. All that is in God is simply divine essence. But the divine essence is imitable by created things in an infinite number of different ways and is known by God as so imitable. Thus we may say that there are in the divine essence an infinite number of what St. Bonaventure calls *similitudines expressivae*, 'creative likenesses', likenesses which are or could be the causes of the existence of an infinite number of particular created things; and this is what the Ideas are.[1] They are thus many Ideas or likenesses but one thing, the divine essence infinitely imitable or communicable. Their multiplicity is a relative multiplicity with respect to the *ideata*, the things which are or could be created in the likeness of the Ideas; and as God is not in any way affected by creatures, creation has no repercussions on God, this relative multiplicity does not involve any real distinction, with the accompanying limitation and imperfection, in the divine essence. God knows the Ideas distinctly and directly. He knows them, that is, not by deducing the knowledge of them as effects from the knowledge of himself as cause, but *simplici aspectu*, in that single and comprehensive regard with which he knows his own infinite essence. The Scholastics, especially St. Bonaventure, are careful to point out how completely this divine knowledge transcends our experience or conceiving. Our minds can only reach towards God's infinite creative thought without ever coming near an adequate apprehension of it.

But this is not the whole story of the transformations which the Platonic World of Ideas, in the form which it took in the philosophy of Plotinus, underwent in Christian

[1]Plotinus, though admitting sometimes the existence of Ideas of individuals, maintained that the number of Ideas was finite, and most pagan Neoplatonists followed him. His senior pupil and assistant, Amelius, however, maintained that the number of Ideas was infinite (cp. Syrianus in Metaph. 147.1ff.).

thought after the conception of the *Logos* as an intermediate being between the Father and creation had been abandoned. Plotinus's divine mind which is the Ideas is not just a mind containing and contemplating a static set of eternal objects. It may be suggested, indeed, that the Forms or Ideas in later Platonism, both Christian and pagan, are never objects in the sense of things set 'over against' the mind which we get to know in the same sort of way in which we get to know a table by seeing it, or a different sort of table by learning it. In the divine mind, or the human mind raised to the divine level (in Plotinus) they are that mind itself eternally known to itself in its own rich fulness; in the human mind thought of as wholly dependent on the divine mind and subject to its gracious influence, they are a kind of illuminative and regulative forces bearing upon it from God (as in St. Augustine and St. Bonaventure). But any full discussion of this very difficult question of the 'objectivity' of the Ideas would be out of place in this chapter and would go far beyond its necessary limits. Plotinus's divine mind, in any case, is not just a mind knowing a lot of eternal objects. It is an organic living community of interpenetrating beings which are at once Forms and intelligences, all 'awake and alive', in which every part thinks and therefore is the whole; so that all are one mind and yet each retains its distinct individuality, without which the whole would be impoverished. And this mind-world is the region where our own mind, illumined by the divine intellect, finds its true self and lives its own life, its proper home and the penultimate stage on its journey, from which it is taken up to union with the Good.

In Christian thought after Nicaea, as we have seen, the Ideas as creative archetypes are in the transcendent Trinity: and the Greek Fathers assert very clearly, unlike

St. Augustine and his successors, that this means that we really cannot in any usual sense know them at all: we have to be taken beyond knowledge to find God. But both the Greeks and St. Augustine retain the idea of a spiritual world, a community of living minds, which is our true home, and of our mind as having a life of its own there into which it must enter as the stage before the last on its ascent to God.[1] In the Christian way of thinking after Nicaea, as we have seen, there is no room for subordinate divinities or intermediaries between Creator and creature. So in the Christian transformation of the thought of Plotinus, just as our self at its highest and truest remains a created being, so the spiritual or heavenly world in which it is at home, no longer identified with the World of Ideas, is a created world. What the Fathers in fact do is to apply as much of what Plotinus says about his intelligible world as can be applied to the highest level of created being, to the heavenly Jerusalem, the City of the Angels, which appears in Christian belief from the earliest times. The Greek Fathers call this the *kosmos noetos*, the intelligible world, and describe its unity in language borrowed from Plotinus, as does St. Augustine, who calls it Created Wisdom, made light by the light of the Uncreated Wisdom, the Word of God.[2] For this Christian transformation of the mind-world of Plotinus is not only a created world. It is a world which owes all its exaltation, all its perfection, all its glory, to the grace of Christ, who is its centre and Lord. And it is a world which, though perfect, is not complete. For all who are to be saved will pass into it till the end of the world, and at the end of

[1] On this development see H. von Balthasar *Présence et Pensée* (Paris, 1942), pp. XVII–XIX, and J. Daniélou *Platonisme et Théologie Mystique* (Paris, 1944), Ch. II, pp. 152–82.
[2] *Confessions*, XII. 15, cp. XII. 11.

the world, at the resurrection, the material universe itself will be transformed into its perfect environment and expression. So it has a history, which the intelligible world of Plotinus, being the world of the eternal archetypes, cannot have. It is, too, a world wholly of persons, whereas the intelligible world of Plotinus is a world which certainly contains persons but of which most of the content is thought of impersonally. This Platonic-Christian conception of the Created Wisdom, the heavenly Jerusalem which is the intelligible world, has deeply influenced Christian thought and worship, especially in the East. Some of its most remarkable expressions are to be found in the works of the great Russian theologians and philosophers, Solovyov and Bulgakov. In the West it has been rather neglected of recent centuries: it is not an idea very easy to fit into either scholastic or Protestant ways of thinking. But in our own times the growing concern with the thought of the Liturgy and the Fathers and the Eastern Christian tradition is leading in some quarters to its revival as an important theological idea,[1] along with much else which belongs to the orthodox Christian mastery and remodelling of Platonism in the fourth and fifth centuries.

[1] The best modern introduction that I know for Western readers to the traditional doctrine of Wisdom is *Le Trône de la Sagesse* by L. Bouyer (Paris, 1957). The principal theme of the book is the mysterious relationship that appears in both Eastern and Western tradition between Created Wisdom and the Mother of God: (this aspect of the tradition has not been touched on here because it has no direct bearing on the question of the influence of Greek philosophy on Christianity). But in describing this he does a great deal to make clear the history and meaning of the whole doctrine of Wisdom, and in particular its deep roots in Jewish tradition, about which I have been able to say very little here.

(E. Tr. *Woman and Man with God*, London, 1960.)

4

The Material Universe

IN the first three centuries of the Christian era, Christians found themselves confronted with a variety of attitudes among their educated pagan contemporaries to the world of which we are aware in sense-experience, the material universe. Of these the most important were the unqualified religious veneration of the material universe as divine which we associate particularly with Stoicism, the Platonic outlook which became dominant in the third century A.D. and was already influential before, and the radical pessimism of the Gnostics. There was also, at least in the first two centuries of our era, a vigorous minority who professed with imperturbable dogmatism the naïve materialism of Epicurus and continued the protest of their master against the veneration of the universe as divine, and all its implications: but it will not be necessary to discuss the Epicureans here, as they were regarded as beyond the pale by all other religious persons (Epicureans were in their own way very genuinely religious) and did not influence the development of Christian thought, though we shall notice one striking coincidence between Epicurean and Christian ways of thinking about the material universe. The other three ways of looking at the universe must, however, be considered carefully, because they (with of course innumerable personal variations and intermediate stages) go to make up the 'climate of opinion' in which the early Christian thinkers worked out their own views of how the teaching of the New Testament about man's relationship to his material environment was to be understood. We begin with what we may call for convenience the 'cosmic religion'.[1] By this term is meant either a religious attitude of mind which regards the cosmos, the material universe in its order and beauty, or at least its highest (in all senses) part, the heavenly bodies and the ether or fire of which they are made, as divine, and the supreme divinity: or an attitude of mind which recognizes some sort of extramundane divinity, but sees the cosmos, and especially the upper cosmos of the heavenly bodies, as the supreme manifestation of divinity and the only way for the mind to ascend to the divine, and for which God is essentially a cosmic god, completely expressed in the cosmos and with no other function except to be its first principle and directing intelligence. The first clear appearance of this cosmic religion in Greek thought is in the later dialogues of Plato, especially Book XII of the *Laws* and the *Epinomis*, or 'Appendix to the Laws' which, if it is not in substance a work of Plato himself (the evidence on this point is not completely decisive), is at any rate a work of the first generation of his Academy. But Platonic religion, as we shall see, was never simply cosmic religion, which owes its full philosophical formulation rather to Aristotle and the Stoics. Its influence was widespread, affecting the minds of many people who adhered to no particular philosophical

[1]A vast amount of very unequal value has been written on this subject. A good and extremely comprehensive recent work is Vol. II of A. J. Festugière's great work *La Révélation d'Hermès Trismégiste. Le Dieu Cosmique.* (Paris, 1949.)

school and extending well beyond the circle of those who had received any tincture of philosophical education, as the studies of F. Cumont have shown:[1] but it was essentially a learned, scientific and (in the later Roman Empire) official religion rather than a genuinely popular one. Its most distinguished and accessible literary monument is that impressive structure of superbly expressed commonplaces the *Somnium Scipionis*, the edifying dream-story which concludes Cicero's *De Republica*.

It is not possible here to discuss all the varying formulations of the cosmic religion which resulted from the interaction of Platonic, Aristotelian, Stoic and Neo-Pythagorean ideas in the period between the third century B.C. and the third century A.D. (they will be found fully discussed in Festugière's book referred to above). We may, however, attempt to summarize those doctrines of the cosmic religion which were common to all schools and widely accepted by educated men of no precise philosophical allegiance, with some indication of the possible variations. According to this way of thinking, the material universe is formed and ordered by a divine intelligence, immanent or transcendent, and is consequently good and beautiful, manifesting the divine intelligence particularly in the order and regularity of its movements. It is the perfect manifestation of the divinity, and is therefore unchangeable as a whole, either everlasting or repeating itself exactly in every detail in an endless series of cycles. Man can only find God in or through the contemplation of the universe, and especially its upper and outer part, the region of the heavenly bodies: for this upper cosmos is generally considered far more good and

[1]See specially his great works on late pagan beliefs about the life after death *Le Symbolisme Funéraire des Romains* (Paris, 1942), and *Lux Perpetua* (Paris, 1949).

beautiful and a better manifestation of God than the lower cosmos, the sublunary world, though the sharpness of the contrast varies. The heavenly bodies and the outer sphere of heaven itself are divine (either the supreme or subordinate divinities). Fire, light, ether, are either the intelligent divine substance or very closely akin to it.

Man's soul is itself of divine nature and substance and, because it is, can contemplate the divinity in the universe and will after death either be re-absorbed into the divine or will return to its proper home in the upper cosmos among the stars (and spend a happy eternity watching them go round). The circular motions and spherical shape of the heavenly bodies are considered far more perfect and beautiful than the irregular shapes and straight-line movements of the beings of our sublunary world (a point of the doctrine which, not unnaturally, amused the Epicureans vastly). In the sharp contrast which is characteristic of the later forms of the cosmic religion between the poor little beings here below in the sublunary world, with their jerky incomplete movements in pursuit of external and unsatisfying ends, in a moist fog of corruption and pollution in the most ignoble place in the universe, and the eternal dance of the immeasurably vast spheres of fire, pursuing their self-contained circuits in the regions above the moon where all is brightness, purity and intelligent order, there is a curious kind of materialized other-worldliness which has had a considerable effect on the minds and imaginations of Europeans in later centuries.

As we have already remarked, the cosmic religion, like so much else that was of importance in later Greek thought, had its origin in Plato: and right down to the end of paganism we find pagan Platonists, Plotinus, Julian, Proclus, Simplicius, vigorously defending its cardinal doctrines, the

eternity of the visible universe and the divinity of the
heavenly bodies, against Gnostics and orthodox Christians.
But none the less the Platonism of the first centuries of the
Christian era regards the material universe in a way which
must be clearly distinguished from the cosmic religion just
outlined. Platonic religion was never merely cosmic religion.
The Platonists remained faithful to the teaching of their
master in maintaining the existence of the transcendent
spiritual world of Forms. The contrast between the material
and spiritual worlds was for Platonists far more important
than that between the upper and lower cosmos. And for
them the supreme object of human intellectual and moral
effort was not simply to return to the stars but to rise to its
proper activity of disembodied contemplation of the Forms
and their first principle, the One or Good: and it was very
much a matter of temperament how much importance a
Platonist attached to the contemplation of the heavenly
bodies as a preliminary approach to the divine. The
greatest of the Platonists, Plotinus, though he produced an
admirable defence of the essentials of cosmic religion against
the Gnostics,[1] certainly did not attach much importance to
it. The way to God for him lay straight from his own soul
through his intellect: his approach was essentially interior,
not from the external world. Further, for Platonists the
material universe as a whole was not absolute perfection,
and the highest conceivable perfection, as it was for the
Stoics. It was only the best possible universe that could be
produced under difficult circumstances. There was and
always remained in it an independent element of unreason
and disorder which the divine intelligence had to bring
under control as best it could. The Platonists of the Empire
certainly never wavered in their conviction that the

[1] *Enneads* II 9 [33].

material universe as a whole was good, beautiful and manifestly the work of the divine intelligence. But they insisted very strongly on the contrast between its necessary imperfection and the perfection of the intelligible world; and they took a strongly other-worldly view of the destiny of man, seeing the sense-world and the life of the senses as a hindrance to the soul, something to be escaped from and transcended; indeed their language at times in this sort of context is not far removed from that of the Gnostics, though their fundamental position remains very different.

The pessimistic Gnostics[1] of course took a thoroughly unfavourable view of the material universe. It is difficult to sum up the endless complexities of their strange, imaginative, and still very imperfectly known systems in any generalization that will be even approximately true: we may perhaps say without radically misrepresenting them that in their view the material universe was something that ought not to have been there at all; it was a great pity that it ever had to occur, because it was the result in some way of the fall of a spiritual being, of sin and ignorance and disorder in the spiritual world, or else (in Manichaeism) of an aggression by the powers of evil against the powers of good. For that select person the true Gnostic (different by nature from the rest of humanity) it was an evil and imprisoning environment from which his secret knowledge enabled him to escape and ascend to the transcendent spiritual world, his true home.

It was in the context of these divergent lines of thought

[1]Among those who speak the language of a secret *gnosis* or saving knowledge there are writers who take a thoroughly positive and optimistic view of the material universe. Several of the pagan gnostic treaties which make up the *Corpus Hermeticum* expound the cosmic religion in a form like that of the pseudo-Aristotelian *De Mundo*, though others are thoroughly pessimistic and dualist.

that the Christians had to work out their own understanding of the outlook on the material universe required by
the Christian revelation. Even without the complications
introduced by late-Hellenistic ways of thinking this would
never have been an easy task. The Christian faith does not
permit any facile and obvious solutions in this matter. And
it was a very great achievement that by the later patristic
period so much that was unsatisfactory in contemporary
thought had been rejected, so much that was valuable had
been taken over and transformed, and the essentials of the
Christian position clearly thought out and stated. The two
extremes, the idolatry of the cosmic religion and the
Gnostic and Manichaean blasphemy against the Creator,
were finally rejected and condemned. We may take as a
classic expression of the essential points of a balanced
Christian teaching about the material universe a passage
from the Christmas sermons of Pope St. Leo the Great
(pope from 440 to 461).[1] St. Leo is here rebuking those
Christians who still turn to salute the rising sun before they
enter St. Peter's. After some extremely vigorous remark
about their behaviour he goes on: 'What is the sun, and
what is the moon? They are only parts of the visible creation, things which give bodily light.' Then follow some
observations on the practical usefulness of the heavenly
bodies, very much in the vein of Hellenistic popular
theodicy, and then St. Leo continues: *Expergiscere, o homo
et dignitatem tuae cognosce naturae. Recordare te factum ad
imaginem Dei; quae, etsi in Adam corrupta, in Christo tamen es
reformata.*

Man, awake, and recognize the dignity of your own
nature. Remember that you were made in the image of

[1] *In Nativitate Domini Sermo* VII (XXVII in Ballerini-Migne).

God; and though it was spoilt in Adam, it has been re-made again in Christ. Use these visible creatures as they ought to be used, as you use earth, sea, sky, air, springs and rivers; and praise and glorify the Creator for every-thing fair and wonderful in them. Do not devote your-self to the light in which birds and snakes, beasts and cattle, flies and worms delight. Feel bodily light with your bodily senses and clasp with all the strength of your mind that true light which 'lightens every man coming into this world' and of which the Prophet says 'Come to him and be enlightened, and your faces shall not be ashamed'. For if we are the temple of God, and the Spirit of God dwells in us, what everyone of the faithful has in his own soul is more than what he admires in the sky. We are not of course, dearly beloved, telling you this to persuade you to despise the works of God, or to think that there is anything against your faith in the things which the good God has made good; but so that you may use every kind of creature, and all the furniture of this world, reasonably and temperately. 'For the things which are seen', as the Apostle says 'are temporal: but the things which are not seen are eternal'. So, since we are born to the things of this present life but reborn to those of the future life, let us not devote ourselves to temporal goods but be set on eternal ones; and, that we may be able to look more closely on our hope, let us consider in this very mystery of the Birthday of the Lord what the grace of God has given to our nature. Let us listen to the Apostle when he says 'For you are dead, and your life is hid with Christ in God. When Christ your life shall appear, then you will appear with him in glory'; who lives and reigns with the Father and the Holy Spirit for ever and ever. Amen.

This may all seem to us straightforward and even
obvious enough, and an authentic echo of the teaching of
the New Testament. But there is a great deal in it which
will repay detailed consideration. First we may note that
St. Leo's insistence that the sun and moon are just material
things, *corporeae lucis elementa*, and that redeemed humanity
surpasses the heavens in dignity and interest, which may
seem to us simple common sense and elementary religion,
would have been profoundly shocking to St. Leo's few
pagan contemporaries, and would have outraged the finest
religious sensibilities of most educated men a couple of
centuries earlier. Even Plotinus, to whom the cosmic religion really meant very little regards a similar claim by the
Gnostics to a kinship with the divine which they deny to
the stars as an intolerable piece of blasphemous arrogance.[1]
This, from the point of view of adherents of the cosmic
religion, was the great blasphemy of which Epicureans,
Gnostics and orthodox Christians were alike guilty. It is
one of the very few points where Epicureans and Christians
agree. We find Lucretius proving on Epicurean principles
against believers in the cosmic religion that the heavenly
bodies cannot be alive and intelligent;[2] for the Epicureans
intelligence is found only in the anthropomorphic gods of
the *intermundia* and in man, so that man is akin to the
divine in a way in which the stars are not.

But St. Leo's way of disposing of the cosmic religion has
deeper and more widely interesting implications. His 'What
every one of the faithful has in his own soul is more than
what he admires in the sky', with what follows, shows us
that interiority, that assertion of the absolute primacy of

[1] *Enneads* II. 9 especially Chs. 9 and 16. Plotinus's general attitude to the material universe in this treatise is in most ways much
more acceptable to a Christian than that of his Gnostic opponents.
[2] V. 122–45.

spirit, which is surely an essential part of any authentic Christian thinking about the material world. God is Spirit, and he comes to us so that we come to him in and through our spirit, and man's spiritual activity as knower and lover of God has an unconditional primacy over his external bodily activities in the sense-world. It was by teaching St. Augustine the nature of spirit and the way to God in the spirit that Plotinus led him back to St. John and St. Paul: and it is the fundamental community of outlook on this point which justifies the use which the Fathers made of Platonism and the continuing influence of Plotinus on Christian thought, though not the exaggerated and distorted other-worldliness into which Christians have sometimes been led by Platonic, though more often by unconscious Gnostic or Manichaean influences (this is discussed in the next chapter). We must not fall into that despising of the good things God in his goodness has made against which St. Leo warns us. But his final quotation from St. Paul reminds us that in some very real sense a death to the things of this world is a necessary condition of Christian life.

The change from cosmic to inward and spiritual religion has important consequences for the Christian attitude to natural science. For the adherents of the cosmic religion natural science either actually was theology, the study of the nature and behaviour of God, as it was for the Stoics, or at least the only way to God conceived as a quasi-spatially transcendent extra-mundane deity who makes the cosmos work from outside and has no other function, but is completely expressed in its order and beauty.[1] But in

[1] cp. Ch. II. This is the conception expressed in the pseudo-Aristotelian *De Mundo* which had a great influence on late pagan thought. It re-appeared again later, and in eighteenth-century Germany was mistaken for the orthodox Christian doctrine of God. See J. Pieper *Wahrheit der Dinge* (Munich, 1948), pp. 48–50.

Christian thought natural science need no longer be confused or integrated into a false synthesis with metaphysics
and theology, and this is to the advantage of both. Metaphysical thinking is recognized as dealing with our experience in a way quite different from that appropriate to
natural science, which is set free to find its own methods and
go its own way because particular physical theories no
longer form part of theology, as they did in the cosmic
religion. Of course the ancient cosmology of the sublunary
world and the ethereal spheres continued for centuries to
be believed in and taken very seriously by Christians and
provided the imaginative setting for their thinking, in
particular about the life after death. We still use, and shall
probably always use, much of the admirable symbolism
which derives from the ancient religious picture of the world,
especially the symbolism of light. And of course ecclesiastical
and academic resentment of the disturbance of established
ideas combined with a falsely literal interpretation of the
Bible could lead to marginal clashes between Church
authorities and scientists, as in the case of Galileo. But the
essential link between physical science and theology was
broken with the turning from cosmic to inward and
spiritual religion (it should be remembered that for the
great majority of simple people in the Mediterranean
world it had never been forged; their gods were simpler
and nearer at hand than the Cosmic Mover and the
heavenly bodies). The acceptance by Christian thinkers of
Plotinus's repudiation of materialistic ways of thinking and
of his 'interior' approach to metaphysics, combined with
their rejection of his clinging to the traditional orthodoxies
of the cosmic religion, has had in the long run the very
satisfactory result that a Catholic Christian philosopher or
theologian can accept any scientific theory that the evidence

seems to require (provided that it is a genuine theory of natural science and not a piece of disguised philosophizing) without its affecting his philosophy or theology in any important way. This is the reason why the final disappearance of the old cosmology as a result of Copernican and post-Copernican developments in astronomy has really made so little difference to orthodox Christian thought. The people who continue to insist that it ought to make all the difference in the world and was in fact a decisive point in the history of our thinking about God and man perhaps do so unconsciously because the change in cosmology provides a good symbol for a change in the outlook on man, nature, and God which came about for quite unastronomical and unscientific reasons.[1]

There is a corollary to all this which may be less pleasing to Christian enthusiasts for the cause of natural science than what has just been said. The way of thinking classically presented by St. Leo surely implies that the study and exploitation of the material universe by the methods of natural science should never be of great importance or interest to the Christian community or to most individual Christians. Natural science is good and legitimate, because the material creation is good, and it may provide the devout scientist with motives for praising God in his works: but it is not on the normal direct route to God. 'Feel bodily light with your bodily senses and clasp with all the strength of your mind that true light . . . what every one of the Faithful has in his soul is more than what he admires in the sky . . . let us not devote ourselves to temporal goods but be set on eternal ones': this is the authentic spirit of the

---

[1] I owe this suggestion to a conversation with that excellent interpreter of English sixteenth and seventeenth century literature and thought, the late Mr. S. L. Bethell.

New Testament, but it is hardly an encouragement to any community or individual to devote the major part of their energy and resources to the pursuit of pure or applied science. The Catholic apologist seems to be justified in pointing out the technical advances and the contributions to the development of scientific theory which were made (generally rather casually and incidentally) in medieval Christendom, and in asserting that in principle the Church gives all legitimate freedom to the scientist. But the anti-Christian scientific humanist also seems to be right in seeing Christian, and in particular Catholic, religion as an obstacle to large-scale rapid scientific progress, unhampered by any serious extra-scientific concerns and inhibitions, which, it appears likely, is only possible in a society where traditional Christianity (or any other of the great religions) has very little real influence.[1]

[1]For a very different view of the proper relationship of science and religion to that given here see P. Teilhard de Chardin, *Le Phénomène Humain* (Paris, 1955: English translation, *The Phenomenon of Man*, London, 1959). Père Teilhard de Chardin had a mind which in its universality of scientific, moral and religious interests resembled that of the great Stoic Posidonius, who probably contributed much to the development of the 'cosmic religion' (though Père Teilhard was a much better scientist and a perfectly orthodox Christian). His book is a most impressive (though to me, and others, not entirely convincing) attempt at a real synthesis of modern scientific thought and traditional Christianity.

5

The Nature and Destiny of Man
Soul and Body

THE Christians came into the Graeco-Roman world with
the passionate conviction that what really mattered to a
man was what happened to him after death, when he went
to God and was judged and would at the end of the world
rise again from the dead to everlasting salvation or damna-
tion: and consequently that what mattered in this life was
to receive the grace of God in Christ and so live in him as
to be approved when he came to judge and share the glory
of his resurrection. Now the only Greek philosophers who
shared in any way the Christian concern with what happened to individual men after death were Platonists and
Pythagoreans and those influenced by the Platonic-
Pythagorean tradition. The Stoics on the whole were
agnostic and indifferent about individual immortality unless, like Seneca, they were deeply influenced by Platonism.
In the normal Stoic view the destiny of the soul, either at
death or at the conflagration which closed the Great Year,
when the divine fire took all things back into itself, was
absorption into the divine substance. The Aristotelians believed in the survival only of the impersonal 'active intellect', the eternal principle which sets our thinking going

(see below Ch. 6), which was identified by the greatest of
Aristotelian commentators, Alexander of Aphrodisias, and
probably by his teacher Aristocles, in the late second and
early third centuries A.D., with God, the first cause, and in
any case was not regarded as a real part of the personality.
Only in the dialogues of Plato and the contemporary teaching of Platonists, and of the adherents of a revived Pytha-
goreanism much influenced by Plato and hardly distin-
guishable from Platonism, could Christians find a doctrine
of the survival of man's self, of his intellectual and moral
personality, of judgement and rewards and punishments in
the hereafter. And though, as we shall see, there are
serious differences between Christianity and Platonism, the
Christians recognized the kinship of their teaching with
Platonism on these very important points, and were influenced by the Platonic view of the nature of man.

But before we go on to discuss the relationship between
Platonic and Christian ideas of man and his destiny in more
detail, a point must be made about Greek philosophy in
general which is required for the proper understanding of
the general relationship between Greek and Christian
thought about the nature and destiny of man. This is that
even those philosophies (Aristotelianism, orthodox Stoicism,
Epicureanism) which denied or were not interested in life
after death and for which life in this world, here and now,
was the only or the only important life, were not 'worldly'.
They did not, that is, regard the acquisition of obvious
worldly goods or advantages, bodily pleasures and com-
forts, wealth, power, rank and honour, for oneself or for
one's community or fellow-men, as the proper object of
human life. They set as man's proper object the acquiring
of virtue and wisdom and preached (and sometimes
practised) poverty and simplicity of life. The ordinary man,

of course, and the ordinary statesman or emperor, was at least as profoundly worldly then as now. Festugière's warning against the falsification of perspective which can result from attending exclusively to the religious and philosophical literature of the first Christian centuries is a very timely one. As he says, 'Human beings, then as now, were solidly attached to the goods of this world, stuck deep in matter. . . . The masses demanded bread and the games of the circus; the rich aspired to luxury and pleasure.'[1] The gay thoroughly worldly mosaics of Piazza Armerina,[2] with their bikini-girls and chariot-races and hunting-scenes, can serve (along with plenty of other evidence of the same kind) as a useful corrective of the impression produced by concentrating too exclusively on the religious and moral teachers, Christian and pagan, of the first centuries of our era. But the philosophers uniformly protested against this worldliness and insisted that bodily and external goods, the *perimachēta agatha*, 'goods men fight about', as Aristotle describes them in a phrase pregnant with meaning,[3] were not worth fighting about after all and were either of no value or of very limited value as compared with the goods of the soul, virtue and wisdom. This attitude to worldly goods among philosophers was independent of any particular philosophical doctrine about the relationship of soul and body or about immortality. It is to be found in a moderate form in Aristotle,[4] and in a rather extreme form in Epicurus

[1] *Révélation d'Hermès Trismégiste* Vol. IV. p. 261.

[2] This magnificent country house in Sicily, recently excavated, was possibly the hunting-box of one of the Emperor Diocletian's colleagues, Maximian Herculius.

[3] *Nicomachean Ethics*, IX 8.1169a, 21.

[4] Aristotle of course maintained that for perfect well-being there was needed that modicum of bodily and family advantages and material goods which a decent Greek gentleman would regard as

and his followers, for whom the soul was an atomic structure dissolved at death; the real Epicureans were ascetic quietists, not the piggish hedonists their enemies made them out to be. The Christians whole-heartedly approved and accepted this philosophical unworldliness, and it was in their eyes one of the greatest virtues of Greek philosophy that it encouraged this frame of mind.

We now come to consider the differences between the pagan Platonists and the Christians about the destiny of man and the relationship of his soul to his body. The pagan Platonists regarded the doctrine of the resurrection of the body as horrible and ridiculous, and their vigorous rejection of it indicates a difference between Platonic and Judaeo-Christian views of the nature of man which goes deep enough, though its extent and implications are often exaggerated and misunderstood. For the Platonists our present earthly, animal body was no real part of ourselves and was more of a hindrance than a help to the soul in the attainment of virtue and wisdom. It was not evil; like the rest of the material creation it was a good and beautiful work of the divine intellect, and we were in it for a good reason, to carry the reign of intellect and soul down to the lowest possible level, and we had duties to it and in the material world which we ought not to shirk. But it was on the whole a nuisance and an encumbrance, and to have to go back

---

essential for a satisfactory life: but the possession of virtue was much more important to him than these modest external requirements. A later philosopher, Antiochus of Ascalon, whose lectures Cicero attended and whose moral teaching he reproduced, attempted a compromise between Aristotle's position and the intransigent Stoic insistence that virtue alone was needed for well-being, by saying that virtue alone could give a *vita beata* but some bodily goods were necessary for the *vita beatissima*.

into it again after being finally released from it seemed to them a depressing future prospect which it was fortunately quite irrational to anticipate. The pagan Platonists regarded the disorder, blindness, weakness, and all hindrances to our spiritual life which we experience here below as necessary consequences of being in an earthly body, which we could not completely escape from (though we might master them) as long as we remained in it. They did however believe that there were other bodies in the material universe which were perfectly subordinated to spirit and did not in any way hinder its life, the heavenly bodies of the upper cosmos; and many of them believed that the ultimate destiny of a perfectly good and wise man was to be embodied in a heavenly body, perfectly conformed and subordinate to his spirit, and not to be altogether disembodied. In Jewish-Christian tradition man is a single whole of which body is just as much a part as soul; and for this way of thinking the resurrection of the body is a natural and inevitable part of any doctrine of the future life. And the evils and impediments to the spiritual life which our present life in the body brings are explained not as natural and inevitable consequences of earthly embodiment but as the result of the Fall of Man, which leaves open the possibility that our Redemption from that fall may bring us to a perfect and glorious life in a spiritualized earthly (in the cosmographical sense) body and not require our transference to a body actually placed in the heavens and made of celestial material. The contrast with the Platonic view, it would seem, could hardly be sharper.[1] But one or two

[1]The most balanced and intelligent of recent Christian discussions of the contrast between dualist and unitary views of man's nature that I know is in the final chapter of Professor R. C. Zaehner's *At Sundry Times* (London, 1958), pp. 173ff. I agree in all essentials with his conclusions.

things must be borne in mind when considering the Christian doctrine which reduce the sharpness of its opposition to Platonism and make it easier to understand the attraction which the Platonist view of man had (and often still has) for philosophically educated Christians. The Christians were from the beginning concerned to refute the absurd and depressing misconception that the life of the resurrection would be a mere reproduction of our present life, with the same needs, desires and activities. This was the misconception of the Sadducees in the Gospel (St. Matthew 22.23ff.),[1] and Christ's answer to them 'In the resurrection they neither marry nor are given in marriage, but are like angels in heaven', set the tone for later orthodox Christian speculation about the risen life. St. Paul too, in the fifteenth chapter of the first epistle to the Corinthians, seems to be concerned to emphasize not only the reality of our risen body but its difference from our present one; this is surely the point of the sharply-drawn anthitheses between *epigeios* or *choikos*, 'earthly' or 'earthy' and *epouranios* 'heavenly', between *psychikos*, 'with a natural principle of life' and *pneumatikos* 'with a spiritual principle of life' which run all through the passage on the resurrection body (35–50). And this sharp contrast between the two lives and the two bodies persists in Christian tradition. The elaborated descriptions of the resurrection-body in the mediaeval scholastics,[2] in which it appears as without natural needs or desires, free from many of our present limitations and

[1] cp. St. Mark 12. 18–27 and the even more striking version of the answer in St. Luke 20.35–37.

[2] A good example is St. Thomas *Contra Gentes*, IV. 83ff. St. Augustine was well aware of the resemblance between the two doctrines, and bases on it a powerful attack on Porphyry's denial of the Resurrection, which he finds inconsistent with the pagan Platonists' own beliefs. See *City of God* X. 29, cp. XXII. 26.

entirely subordinated to spirit, though their ultimate source is the Gospel descriptions of the risen body of Christ, have a good deal in common with and probably owe a good deal to the Neoplatonic accounts of astral or celestial bodies; though the Christian theologians insist that the resurrection bodies will be real human bodies, however spiritualized and transformed, and not properly astral or celestial bodies, thus remaining faithful to the Jewish-Christian tradition and avoiding a complete slipping back into the spatial other-worldliness of the cosmic religion (St. Thomas's view in *Contra Gentes* IV. 87 that our resurrection-bodies, though not celestial bodies, will be spatially situated 'above all the heavens' is a curious testimony to the persisting influence of this spatial other-worldliness, but is not, it need hardly be stated, the official teaching of the Catholic Church). A further, and more important point, is that the Christian acceptance of the body as a real and essential part of man does not mean an acceptance of worldliness. If we are to be, as Christ said, 'like angels', even if embodied angels, in the resurrection, we must prepare ourselves for that state by living as spiritually here as the needs and duties proper to our present state will let us; and Christian thinkers, till very recently, have not found the doctrine of the resurrection of the body an obstacle to accepting the judgement of the ancient philosophers about the relative values of the goods of the body and the goods of the soul already referred to; in fact sometimes the sharpness of the distinction they have drawn between the two bodies and the two lives seems to have intensified their other-worldliness to a degree beyond that of any ancient Platonist.

The Christians, then, were able to feel that they had a good deal in common with the Platonists in spite of their deep divergence from them over the resurrection of the

body. As a result, the first Christian thinkers accepted many
of the essential features of Platonic psychology and theory
of knowledge. They were reluctant to admit that the body
had any positive contribution to make to our higher intellectual and religious activities, and tended to regard it as a
hindrance rather than a help to knowing and loving God.
This is not the place to discuss this side of Christian Platonism at length. It is dealt with in the next chapter. But it is
perhaps appropriate to say here that the preoccupation of
Christian as well as pagan Platonists in this part of their
thinking were at least as much ethical as properly psychological. They were concerned, that is, at least as much with
a proper scale of values and a right ordering of human life
as with giving an accurate account, true to experience, of
the relationship of body and soul in human knowing, de-
siring and willing. The body was allowed very little in
psychological theory so that it might be kept firmly in its
proper place when they came to ethical theory and the
practical ordering of their lives. When a pagan or Christian
Platonist spoke of the soul being bound to or dominated by
body in a way contrary to its nature and hampering to its
activities what he had in mind was not the simple fact of
having a body and receiving information from the senses
about the material world. Nor was he thinking, first and
foremost, about paying proper attention to the body's real
needs and the duties of earthly life, in doing which the soul
was performing its godlike function of bringing light and
order into its own part of the visible world. The Christians,
because of their insistence on the love of our neighbour,
certainly stressed the importance of these duties, an expression for them of supernatural *agape* and not only of a just
philanthropia, more than the pagans. But at least the greatest
of the pagan Neoplatonists, Plotinus, neither taught that they

should be neglected nor neglected them himself.[1] What the Platonist really had most in mind was being enslaved to desires for material things and blinded to man's true nature and end by those desires and the strength of our sense-perceptions; being enslaved by lust, greed, avarice and ambition and blinded by ignorance and illusion, and a prey to the hatred and fear that come from these and lead to acts of cruelty and cowardice, to tyrannies and wars and quarrels and disunion of all kinds. The Christians more than the pagans emphasized that bodily desires were contrary to the love of our neighbour as well as to the love of God, but Plotinus still kept the insight which led Aristotle to call material goods 'the goods men fight about'.[2] This ethical emphasis certainly led to some distortion and disregard of experience in Christian Platonist psychology. But when St. Thomas Aquinas adopted a more Aristotelian (though not a completely Aristotelian) psychology as being more philosophically satisfactory and closer to experience he did not depart in any significant way from the old scale of values, the estimation of the relative importance of the goods of body and soul held by the great Christian Platonist thinkers of whom the chief was St. Augustine.[3]

To prevent some common misunderstandings, it is necessary to say here that Platonism is not the origin of that neurotic obsession with sexual sin, with all its pruderies, repressions and perversions, which is so common and unattractive a feature of puritanical, ascetic and otherworldly interpretations of Christianity, Catholic as well as

[1] Porphyry, *Life*, Ch. 9.
[2] The ultimate source of this idea is Plato. It appears clearly in *Phaedo*, 66C5–D3.
[3] cp. The very clear statement of the traditional position in *Contra Gentes*, II. 79. *Perfectio autem animae humanae consistit in abstractione quadam a corpore.* . . .

Protestant. This cannot spring, as some modern Catholic writers assert (and I used to believe until I examined the evidence more carefully) from Platonism because it is not in the Platonists. For Plato and Plotinus[1] sexual[2] passion is a first manifestation of an *eros* which, rightly directed, can lead us on to God, and in no way something to be merely repressed and condemned. Avarice and the greed for power which makes men tyrants are far more deadly manifestations of body-dominated worldliness than is lust. And there is no good evidence that obsession with sexual sin in Christians increases in proportion as their minds are influenced by Platonism. It is to be found at its worst in the anti-philosophical Tertullian, and in many later writers who share his hostility to philosophy. The great Christian Platonists, St. Augustine or St. Gregory of Nyssa, though sometimes excessively severe and negative about sex and marriage, are far more balanced than Tertullian and the anti-intellectual moralist-preachers who follow in his tradition. And in our own time it is certainly not among those Christians who still draw religious and moral inspiration from the works of Plato and Plotinus that this sort of depraved prudery is most in evidence. A psychiatrist would probably be a better person to consult about its origins than a historian of ideas. But if historical reasons are to be suggested for its appearance and prevalence, one might sug-

[1] cp. the admirable summary of the teaching of Plato's *Symposium* and *Phaedrus* in Plotinus's treatise *On Dialectic* I 3 [20] 2.

[2] If anyone wishes to substitute 'homosexual', and try to discredit Platonism on these lines, he will be well advised first to study *all* the relevant Platonic passages, with the help of good modern commentaries (e.g. Hackforth's *Phaedrus*), including the passage in Laws VIII. 836 A ff. where Plato denounces unnatural vice with a vigour worthy of a Father of the Church: and to remember how profoundly shocked Plotinus was by an attempt to defend philosophical paederasty (Porphyry, *Life*, Ch. 15).

gest, first, an exaggerated reaction from the public and unashamed sexual licence of the ancient world and particularly from the close connexion of sexuality and religion in certain cults: and then the unconscious influence of Gnostic and, still more, Manichaean ideas, from which Platonists and orthodox Christians were by no means always exempt. In judging the literary evidence, too, attention should be paid to the universal tendency of ancient moralizers to rhetorical exaggeration and to the popular anti-feminism, expressed in coarse and violent satire, which was so widespread in the ancient world.

Still less should *Platonic* other-worldliness be made responsible for that hostility to the beauties of nature and art as a snare for the spirit, or indifference to them as of no religious value, which is often to be found among puritanical and other-worldly Christians, of all periods and denominations. Plotinus's profound, magnificent and thoroughly positive reflections on the beauty both of nature and of art are, or should be, well known; they have deeply influenced later European thought and, perhaps, artistic practice.[1] And for both pagan and Christian Platonists the beauty perceived by our senses was an expression, a sign, a sacrament in the wide sense of the greater beauty of the invisible world, and so not only good but holy, of real religious value. The Neoplatonists and at least the older Christian tradition in fact share a view of all bodily and earthly things which is neither a complete acceptance of them as ends in themselves and sufficient objects of our love

[1] A fairly good idea of his thought about beauty can be gathered from the selections translated in my *Plotinus* (London, 1953), pp. 144–9. Two good recent books are E. de Keyser, *La Signification de l' Art dans les Ennéades de Plotin* (Louvain, 1955), and Fiammetta Bourbon di Petrella, *Il Problema dell'Arte e della Bellezza in Plotino* (Florence, 1956).

or a complete rejection of them as evil and hindrances to our spiritual life, but a sacramental view, an acceptance of the things that are visible as signs of and helps on the way to God and his hidden kingdom; a view which accords perfectly with that understanding of the Incarnation expressed in the Preface of Christmas in the Roman Liturgy *ut dum visibiliter Deum cognoscimus, per hunc in invisibilium amorem rapiamur:* 'that while we acknowledge Him to be God seen by men, we may be carried away by Him to the love of things unseen'.[1] It was because the Christians came to share this sacramental outlook on the things of this world that Greek thought was able to achieve its greatest triumph, against the strongest opposition, within Christianity; this was the definite and whole-hearted acceptance by the Catholic Church of East and West in the eighth and ninth centuries of the veneration of holy images. Those Christians who accept the development of the veneration of the saints and angels in the Church as a true development, in essentials at least, guided by the Holy Spirit, and not as a monstrous corruption, must if they are honest, see in it a justification of Plotinus's great protest against the narrow-minded Christian polemic of his day which ends 'Those who really know the power of God do not contract the divine into one, but display it as manifold, as he himself has displayed it, inasmuch as, abiding who he is, he makes many gods, all depending upon him and existing through him and from him'.[2] And when the long-standing controversy about the veneration of images of Christ and the saints came to a head in eighth century Byzantium, it was Platonic arguments about the

[1] Translation from the *St. Andrew Daily Missal.*

[2] *Enneads* II, 9 [33] 9. For the use of 'the divine' and 'gods' here cp.: the remarks on the meaning of *theos* in Ch. III. Professor C. S. Lewis sometimes refers to angelic beings as 'gods' in his novels without any detriment to his perfectly orthodox monotheism.

relation of image to archetype, implying that whole sacramental view of the relation of visible to invisible just referred to as their background, which were used by the ultimately victorious defenders of the holy images. They were in fact to a great extent the same arguments which had been used by the pagan Neoplatonists in defending themselves against Christian charges of idolatry:[1] so in their acceptance (and continued use ever since) by the Church we must again see a belated justification of the Neoplatonist standpoint. It was, of course, only a limited justification of these particular arguments, not of Neoplatonist, still less of ordinary Hellenic, paganism as a whole. There were plenty of genuine polytheists in the ancient world even though Plotinus was not one, and perhaps even some genuine idolaters (though *real* idolatry, which identifies the image with the god, seems to be a rather rare phenomenon). And there was plenty, as has been already shown, in Neoplatonist philosophical religion which was really incompatible with Christianity.

But however Platonic the psychology of some Christians may have become, and however much they may have accepted the Platonic view of the body, there was one individual development of Platonic psychology which they never accepted or could accept. This was the 'double personality' psychology of Plotinus, his distinction of the 'man within' and the 'other man', according to which our true self is an eternal intelligent soul which does not 'come down', which cannot sin or suffer, repent or be saved; sin and suffering belong to the lower self, the 'other man', the

---

[1]On Hellenic philosophical religion and the Iconoclast controversy see N. H. Baynes *Idolatry and the Early Church* in *Byzantine Studies* (London, 1955), pp. 116–43, a most distinguished and convincing study on which this paragraph is based.

inferior soul (a *logos* or expression of the higher on a lower plane of being) which forms a composite entity with body. This doctrine is peculiar to Plotinus, and should not be described as 'Platonic' or 'Neoplatonic' without qualification. The later pagan Neoplatonists not only abandoned but vigorously repudiated it, and adopted a unitary and humbler view of the human soul which was perhaps nearer to Plato's real thought and certainly more acceptable to a Christian. Plotinus's thought here, though its ultimate origin is certainly in the intellectualism of Plato, derives at least as much from Aristotelianism as from Platonism. Plotinus seems to have been influenced by what he read in Alexander of Aphrodisias[1] about the Active Reason which continues its everlasting activity quite unaffected by what happens to the soul in which for the time it is present, and perhaps too by that sharp psychological dualism, that separation of the intellect, the 'true self' from the moral personality, which is to be found in Aristotle's *Nicomachean Ethics* in Books IX and X—Plato never makes this separation of the intellectual and moral personalities; our highest and truest self for him always remains morally responsible, and is never a pure intellect beyond moral activity.[2] It is

[1]*Mantissa*, p. 112. 18–113.2. Bruns. For a discussion of this passage and its probable influence on Plotinus see my paper in *Entretiens Hardt*, V (Vandoeuvres, 1960).

[2]I am not of course suggesting that the *nous* (intellect) of the rather rough-and-ready popular psychology of the *Ethics* is to be identified with the *nous choristos* (the 'separable', called by later Aristotelians, the 'active' intellect) of the 'scientific' psychology of the *De Anima*. Plotinus when he uses the Aristotelian term *nous choristos* applies it, not to the higher soul, but to the divine intellect on the level of which the higher soul continually lives. And Plotinus's account of the human personality is both more subtle and more unified than that given by Aristotle in either the *Ethics* or the *De Anima*. He is the greatest psychologist of antiquity, and his ideas in some ways anticipate modern psychological discoveries.

worth noticing that the higher self in the later and fully developed form of Plotinus's doctrine is not identical with our eternal archetype in the Divine Intellect. It is a higher *soul*, illumined and maintained eternally in the higher world by Intellect. Now this doctrine in which the true self, our real I, needs no salvation because it cannot sin and enjoys eternally the divine attributes of impeccability and impassibility, seems quite incompatible with Christianity. The Christian can, indeed must, admit that the archetypal self of which he is the image exists eternally in Christ, who conforms him to it by his redeeming grace, so that there is a very real sense in which Christ is 'more my self than myself'. But he cannot admit that he, the real he, is by nature beyond and incapable of sin and suffering, above all change and instability.

This doctrine is perhaps the most radically anti-Christian part of the thought of Plotinus, and when we turn to his great Christian contemporary Origen, and to the Christian Platonist Fathers of the next centuries, to St. Augustine and St. Gregory of Nyssa, we find that their thought on this subject is essentially different and sharply opposed. They insist, in different ways but all with the utmost emphasis, on the essential instability of all created beings, their liability to sin, and their continual need of God's grace. This applied even to the highest created spiritual beings, to the *kosmos noetos* or Created Wisdom, the world of the angels. Every angel could fall, and some angels have fallen. Instability, the real possibility of change, runs through all creation from lowest to highest.[1] In thinking like this the Christian Platonists were not just trying to be different from the pagan Plotinus. They thought in this

[1]For a fuller discussion, see my paper 'Salvation Plotinian and Christian' in *Downside Review*, Spring, 1957, pp. 126–39.

way, and transformed the elements of Plotinus's thought which they took over to fit in with this way of thinking, because they were Christians. Here, as in the development of the theology of the Trinity described in Ch. 3 we can see that instinctive independence and masterfulness which we always find in the greatest and most orthodox Christian thinkers when they are dealing with Greek philosophy. They learn a great deal from it, and are deeply influenced by it, but they are never merely subservient and acquiescent. They stand on their own ground and keep their Christian independence and their primary loyalty to the sources of Christian revelation.

6

Knowing and Understanding

IN trying to assess what Christian thinkers took from the
Greeks in their reflection on knowledge, and what they
made of it, we must first take note of the fact that we
cannot speak either of a 'Greek' or a 'Christian' theory of
knowledge. There are important differences between Plato
and his disciple, Aristotle, on this point, as there were between Plato and Pythagoras, from whom he had certainly
inherited much. And there were other theories—in fact
each school of thought had its theory of knowledge:
Atomists, Stoics, Neoplatonists, sometimes with affinities to
one or other, but with no fundamental identity of concern
to enable us to speak of a 'Greek view of knowledge'. And
not only was there no one Greek view of knowledge, but a
whole multiplicity of views: but also, it is fair to say, there
was no Christian view at all, to begin with. The Bible is
simply not interested in questions of this sort. It is neutral
as between alternative theories of knowledge, and this goes
for Old and New Testaments alike. Thus, when Christians
began to indulge in philosophical speculation, when they
began to draw on the philosophical ideas current in the
Greek world of their time in order to deepen their insight
into the content of their faith, the field was clear before

them. They could pick and choose what seemed best and most illuminating to them, and pick and choose they did. It would be quite impossible in one short chapter to survey, however inadequately, the history of how they went about this; there is far too great a variety both of Greek views and of Christian thinkers. In any case, not a very great deal of the whole range of Greek thought was destined to be of great historical importance, so far as this question is concerned. Stoicism lingered on for a while, and had a certain vogue among some of the early Christian writers.[1] Tertullian alone made a serious attempt to embody its materialistic approach to knowledge in the framework of a Christian philosophy; but somehow the Stoic theory of knowledge proved to be too hard to swallow, and gradually and quietly dropped out. So instead of trying to follow anything like a chronological order, I shall focus attention on the two theories of knowledge which were both the most outstanding in importance for Greek philosophy, and which were to prove the most important for Christian thought. They are of course Plato's and Aristotle's views. The first, seen through the eyes of a good many intermediaries, became very popular in the early Church. We shall look at the way that Plato's views were assimilated by Christian thought in the person of St. Augustine. The other type of view, that associated with Aristotle, did not come into its own in Christian thinking until much later; and when it did, at the hands of the thirteenth-century scholastics like St. Albert the Great and St. Thomas Aquinas, it did so at the cost of a good deal of opposition, distrust and tension. To see what happened to the Aristotelian theory of knowledge when taken up into Christian thinking, we shall look at

[1]On the influence of Stoicism, see M. Spanneut, *Le stoïcisme des Pères de l'Église* (Paris, 1957).

the shape it assumed in the hands of St. Thomas Aquinas.

To start with Plato's theory of knowledge, then, the first thing to note is that for Plato, and the tradition in which he stood, only what was changeless and permanent was strictly speaking knowable. Plato was not, of course, the first to follow this line of thought. Parmenides and some of his followers had pressed it to its limits—so much so that they found all our usual beliefs about the world infected with contradiction, and the appearances of things therefore to be rejected as illusory. But the really great achievement of Greek thought before Plato, and the one which seems to have made an indelible impression on subsequent Greek thinking, including Plato's, was the discovery associated with the name of Pythagoras: the discovery that mathematics can serve as a clue to the natures and the behaviour of things. Pythagoras appears to have discovered this far-reaching principle in studying the properties of audible sounds. He discovered that the pitch of the sound emitted by a vibrating string is proportional to the length of the string. And, even more important, he found out that certain intervals of proportions resulted in concordant sounds, others in discord—in other words, he had found a way of translating into the language of mathematics what was a matter of sense-experience and of feeling. His disciples, Plato among them, may have been a little too sanguine in their hopes of unravelling all the secrets of the cosmos with the aid of this discovery; but it taught them that to grasp the nature of things, we have to look at their structure, of which a mathematical account can be given, rather than at the stuff they are made of, as earlier Greek thinkers had tried to do. What was genuinely knowable is not change, process, and the things which undergo change, but the structure, form and pattern which govern the process.

Mathematical understanding, and geometry in particular, took pride of place in the Pythagorean discovery; but there was no reason why the claims of knowledge should be exhausted in mathematical types of knowledge. Hence when Socrates claimed that moral 'forms' were just as understandable, just as fixed, permanent and eternally valid as mathematical forms and truths, he carried the same line of thought into wider fields. At any rate, notwithstanding the gulf which in many respects separates Socrates from the Pythagoreans, in Plato's mind the Pythagorean and Socratic inheritance blended into a unitary vision of a world of forms, arranged in an ordered hierarchy, which were the objects of knowledge, and distinguished from the world of appearance.

In looking at Plato's theory of forms, and the theory of knowledge which is part of it, we must remember at the outset that this theory, the core of his philosophy, appears at different stages of his thought, with different emphases in different works. Over these nuances my account will have to ride roughshod. It is also beyond our scope to discuss the various views which have been taken of the theory, and of its sources; much of what I shall have to say about this would not be accepted by many scholars—but the same goes for most things one would say on this topic. What Plato inherited from the Pythagoreans, was their stress on mathematical knowledge, and the far-reaching claims for its scope that they had made. The Pythagorean school was much more than a school of philosophers. It was something very much like a religious community, with strict rules of life of its own. One of their most important tenets was that the human soul was of divine origin, that it rightfully belonged to another world, from which it was temporarily banished and housed in a body as a punishment. The pur-

pose of the way of life laid down in the rules of the Pythagorean community was to secure their release from this
life, and release from perpetual return to it in successive
reincarnations. This was quite a novel conception in Greece,
but it seems to have been accepted by Plato. It is easy to see
what happens when you put these two views together. If
you say that knowledge is of forms, not of this world of
change and becoming, and that the soul, whose distinctive
activity is knowing, belongs by right to another world, the
result is that you are tempted to say that the forms belong
to another world. You make yourself a picture of a kind of
divine world of changeless, timeless, intelligible realities,
among which the disembodied soul is really at home. This
is, no doubt, a crude parody of Plato; but something like it,
is I think, what has happened.

As a result of this kind of thinking, what one finds in
Plato's developed thought is something which went well
beyond Socrates, so far as we can tell. Socrates was content
to seek the unchanging, fixed definitions of moral concepts
like 'courage', 'virtue', perhaps even the 'good'. But in
Plato's hands the quest for the knowledge of forms became
a quest of another and more real world. Plato returns to the
old-fashioned conception of the philosopher's function, the
conception which Socrates appears to have repudiated:
that of the philosopher as a kind of prophet or seer, with
access to a hidden world, whose vision can only be expressed in poetry and myth. The extraordinary achievement
of Plato is that he managed to take so much of the concern
for this visible world, and the analytical skill brought to its
understanding by Socrates, with him in his furthest pro-
phetic flights.

This vision inevitably involved a theory of knowledge
for which the liability of perceptible things to change is an

indication of their relative unreality. They are both at the mercy of external forces, and they change without external agency: they are inherently transitory. They are not wholly, completely, what they are, all at once, they are 'becoming', not 'being'. This is the only sense in which they are 'unreal': in calling material things 'unreal', Plato does not mean that when you say 'there is a tree out there' you are mistaken, and there is nothing there. What he means is that the thing which is there is not through and through, essentially and eternally a tree, but a thing subject to the vicissitudes of time and change. It is in a sense contrasted with this that the forms are 'real': they are wholly and unchangeably what they are. This is, of course, clearest in the case of mathematical and geometrical forms, whence, of course, the concept took most of its value. The circle I draw on the board contains many elements of non-circularity; but the geometer's circle is the real, completely circular circle, containing no qualities other than that of its ideal circularity. Plato found confirmation of this theory in the relativity of our sense-experience of perceptible things: they look one shape from one point of view, another shape from another point; they feel now hot, when my hand has been in cold water, then cold; big from near by and small far away, and so on. Perception therefore, he concluded, gives us belief about things—belief could be true or false, it was not all illusion; but to give genuine knowledge, sense-perception was incompetent to do. Knowledge is a prerogative of the mind, of understanding: in its judgement alone is knowledge to be found. This knowledge itself is not of the changing, mutable things we experience; but of the intelligible world of forms. Knowledge of this world is, of course, relevant to the world of becoming: for the things we perceive in this changing, transitory world, 'share in' or 'imitate' the forms, to use the two alternative ways in which Plato speaks of their relation. But the knowledge of forms, relevant though it may be to the world of becoming, cannot be got from it. Knowledge is something which the soul brings with it, from its life among the eternally unchanging forms. Sometimes Plato describes it as knowledge 'remembered' by the soul, that is to say brought with it from a previous state of existence, beyond the bonds of the body and matter.

Plato explains the relation between the forms and the perceptible world, and the parallel relation of knowledge to opinion, by a series of analogies, some of which, despite widely varied interpretations and different ways of being applied, have become classical in the subsequent development of philosophy.[1] In the analogy of the 'line' (*Republic*, V.509–11) Plato displays diagrammatically the different kinds of states of mind with their corresponding classes of objects: a line is divided into two unequal parts, the lower being shorter, to indicate the inferiority of the visible world to the intelligible world. Each part is again sub-divided into two parts, in the same proportion as the whole line, in such a way that $A + B : C + D = A : B = C : D$.[2]

Each of these proportions expresses a relation analogous to the relation between the two lowest divisions of the line, that of C to D, the relation of visible things to their shadows or images and of the corresponding states of mind. The

[1]On the various interpretations of Plato's 'line', 'sun', etc., see: J. L. Stocks, 'The divided line of *Plato, Rep. vi*', in *Class. Q.*, 5(1911), pp. 73–88; A. S. Ferguson, 'Plato's simile of light' in *Class. Q.*, 15(1921), pp. 131–52. 'The allegory of the Cave', in *Class. Q.*, 16(1922), pp. 15–28, and 'Plato's simile of light again', in *Class. Q.*, 28(1934), pp. 190–210; N. R. Murphy, 'Back to the Cave', *ibid.*, pp. 211–13; H. W. B. Joseph, *Knowledge and the good in Plato's Republic* (Oxford, 1948), Chs. 3 and 4: W. F. R. Hardie, *A study in Plato* (Oxford, 1936), Ch. vi, and most other commentators.

[2]See the diagram on p. 66.

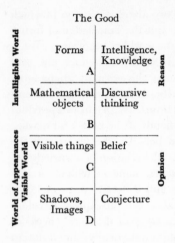

whole visible world is related to the whole intelligible world in a way analogous to this: the visible world is a kind of shadow or image of the intelligible world, on which it depends for its being as a shadow or image does on its original (A + B : C + D = C : D). The intelligible world itself, however, is divided into two parts. The upper line corresponds to forms seen in their dependence on the ultimate source, the form of the Good; the lower section (B) corresponds to forms lower in the hierarchy of forms, not known directly in their relation to the Good. The most typical examples of these appear to be the objects of mathematical thinking. Plato seems to suggest that their dependence on the higher forms is analogous in some way to his basic image-original relation, C : D, so that A : B = C : D. In each case the relations between the states of mind corresponding to each kind of object is similarly analogous to the relation between direct vision of an object and 'imagination' or 'conjecture' based on a shadow or reflection (C : D). Thus intuitive knowledge or intelligence is related to discursive thinking in an analogous fashion (A : B = C : D), and so is the whole field of 'reason' to the whole field of 'opinion' (A + B : C + D = C : D).

The closely relevant analogy of the 'Sun' had a long future before it. This draws attention to the role of the sun with regard to sight and its objects: and the role of the Good with regard to knowledge and its objects: just as the sun, supremely visible in its own right, renders other things visible to the eye, so the Good, supremely intelligible in itself, renders the other forms intelligible to the mind. And Plato stresses that the dependence of the forms on the Good, as of physical things on the sun, is not only in the order of knowledge, but also in that of being.

When we turn to St. Augustine, it is well to remind ourselves of the fact which stares us in the face in almost all his mature writings: that they are the work of a man who has been shaken to the inmost depths of his being. His philosophy—if we can properly speak of a 'philosophy' where we have to do with something at once so personal and so 'theological'—is a kind of intellectual formulation of his autobiography. In his *Confessions* he describes the books of the Platonists, that is to say the Platonic philosophy as it reached him through several hands, as the instrument whereby he was liberated from his earlier, materialistic errors. And even after his conversion to the Incarnate Word of God confessed by the Christian Church, it was in Platonism that he found the best intellectual equipment for gaining deeper insight into truth. There is already an important difference here between Plato and Augustine's Platonism: it is the priority of faith to reason, to all other mental activity. In this, no doubt, we can discern Augustine's despair of ever discovering truth, from which it was his faith that delivered him. Faith, for Augustine, remained the first step on the way to truth, and it is in this sense that we can assert its priority to reason. It gave the mind the direction, provided the goal for its intellectual quest. But though it is prior to reason in this sense, it is not, for Augustine, superior to it. On the contrary: understanding is a higher way of knowing, because when we understand something, we penetrate its nature, so to speak, by an intellectual insight; whereas in *mere* faith this insight is wanting; faith is simply adherence to its object. Hence Augustine speaks of understanding as the goal of faith, or as its reward. 'Believe in order that you may understand' is his often reiterated exhortation (e.g. *Sermo* 43.3.4; cf. *de Trin.* IX.1.1, and countless other passages). What he has in mind when speaking of understanding in such terms is, of course, the fuller penetration into the content of faith, that is to say knowledge of God; and the intellectual quest for expanding the confused and fragmentary knowledge of faith is only completed in the vision of God granted in eternal life. Philosophy—or reason, to use a word that begs fewer questions—is the means of gaining this increased insight; but to get anywhere at all, it must be set in the framework of faith. If one understands this it is easy to see why, in spite of Augustine's closeness to Platonism, there is also an infinite gulf between the two; and why Augustine could see in Platonism both a great liberating force and a means of achieving intellectual insight, and yet, so often, repudiate it in the name of Christianity.

Philosophy, for Augustine, is love of wisdom: beginning in faith, continued in an intellectual quest of insight and crowned by the vision of union. This is the context of his theory of knowledge. Let us turn to this intermediate stage, the intellectual quest itself. All knowledge, whether it is that of sense-perception or of discursive thinking or of intuitive insight, is, for Augustine, an act of the soul. Let us, for a moment, take another look at Plato's line. This analogy suggests that the lower divisions of the line—perceptible things—are in some way 'known' by sense, the higher by reason. Between the two there is nothing in common, and there can be no bridge between them beyond the fact that perceptible things are in fact modelled on the invisible forms by the divine craftsman, and it is these forms that are known by reason. This lack of any direct relation of sense and reason did, I think, worry Plato, and there are indications that he tried to surmount it; but none the less, I don't think I am being grossly unfair in the picture I have given of his view. Augustine cannot quite accept this inaccessibility of the world of sense to reason; he wants to say that reason does know perceptible things, and knows them precisely *through* sense. We shall see in a moment what kind of difficulties he runs into. Man is, according to his definition, a 'rational soul using a mortal and material body' (*de mor. eccl.* I.27.52). Now in sense-perception, what happens is that some external physical process impinges on the appropriate sense-organ of my body: say a ray of light reflected from the surface encounters my eye. The physical thing affects my eye, that is to say my body; there is something going on in me as a result of what is going on outside me. This encounter is perception. But this is where Augustine comes up against a difficulty: the encounter of object and sense-organ will not amount to perception unless I notice it; that is to say, unless it somehow enters my mind. But it is axiomatic for him that the mind cannot be affected by anything of bodily nature, because body is inferior in the scale of beings to mind, and nothing inferior, so he held, could act on a superior thing. So although he is very emphatic that sense-perception is an act of the soul through the body, it is very difficult to see how such an act is possible on his view. The way in which he gets over this difficulty is by suggesting that although the body cannot act on the soul and hence cannot give rise to a sense-perception in the soul, the soul can, and does act on the body. What it does in the case of sense-perception is precisely to take notice of changes in the body as a result of the action of external things on it. The soul, according to this view, is a kind of spiritual presence pervading the whole body, to which everything that goes on in the body is transparent.[1]

It is along such lines that Augustine tries to bridge the gulf between knowledge and the physical world which he inherited from Plato. It is not a very satisfactory solution; thinkers of the Aristotelian tradition were keenly aware of its unsatisfactory nature. We shall see how they tried to deal with this problem later on. But before we come to that, we must complete our picture of the Augustinian theory of knowledge.

Sense-perception, the lowest stage of knowledge, belongs then, like the higher levels, to the mind. The mind is active, not passive in perception: this activity is a bridge to its activity in thinking. Here Augustine is in some ways much closer to Plato than he is in his treatment of sense-perception. For Plato, as we saw, the objects of the mind in thinking are mathematical objects and forms. The knowledge which the mind has of these, is derived from its recollection of them from a previous state of existence, when it was at home among the forms. Augustine, after some initial hesitation, was led to reject this theory, as the pre-existence of souls is not an acceptable Christian view. But fundamentally, from a philosophical point of view, his solution is very similar: the forms—now ideas in the divine mind—yield their eternal truth to the mind in the light of a divine illumination in the mind. This is an exact replica of Plato's image of the sun: for Augustine, too, God is to the mind what the sun is to the things visible to the eye. In the light

[1] cp. E. Gilson, *Introduction à l'étude de saint Augustin* (Paris, 1929), Ch. iv, for an excellent account of Augustine's theory of sense-knowledge.

which is in the mind, the mind's objects become intelligible
to the mind just as sunlight renders material things visible.
The spiritual light is the mind's participation in the Word
of God, and sometimes Augustine speaks of this light as the
Interior Teacher, Christ dwelling in the soul and teaching it
from within.

This is a very rough and ready account of a doctrine that
was very dear to Augustine, to which he often came back
in different ways, and to which he gave a good deal of
subtle thought. I am afraid my crude summary must, however, suffice.[1]

Before we leave Augustine, there is one further point I
should just like to touch on. If one tries to fit Augustine's
theory of knowledge into the scheme of Plato's line, one
finds that the correspondence has broken down. Augustine
isn't interested in the subdivisions; he has no mathematical
axe to grind, and for him there is no important distinction
to be drawn between mathematical and other eternal
truths. And yet, for him too, reason, the upper portion of
the line, is divided.[2] His distinction is between what he calls
a 'higher' and a 'lower' reason. But the distinction isn't
between two different mental processes or faculties; it is
between two different functions of one and the same
faculty, reason. The higher reason is reason at work on
divine truth, the lower is reason at work on human and
material things. The parallel distinction is that between
wisdom—the specific excellence achieved by the mind in
dealing with divine things, and knowledge or science, its

---

[1] I have drawn attention to some of these divergences in my
article 'St. Augustine on signs', in *Phronesis*, 2 (1957), pp. 60–83;
see particularly pp. 69–70, 81–82.

[2] This is to a great extent also true of Plotinus: he, too, distinguishes between νοῦς and διανοία (which is a function of ψυχή),
and does so more sharply than Augustine.

specific excellence achieved in dealing with lower things. On this distinction between 'science' and 'wisdom' Augustine builds some of his most far-reaching thought on the role of speculation in human life.

Going back now to Aristotle, we find an interesting continuation of the Platonic line of thought, which is, at the same time, a criticism of it. There is, first of all, a whole set of acute arguments against Plato's separation of the forms, that is to say aimed against his view of the objects of knowledge as being 'laid up in heaven' and as genuinely different entities from the perceptible objects all around us in the world, which are modelled on the forms. We cannot go into these criticisms now, but we must very briefly look at what Aristotle substitutes for Plato's view. In his account of the world, the individual concrete things are what is 'really real'; there is no heaven of intelligible substances placed over against the world of becoming and passing away. The forms are brought firmly back into the world of experience. They inhere in the concrete things of which this world is composed, and their correlative is what Aristotle calls 'matter'. Neither form nor matter are capable of existing by themselves. Form is the principle of organization, of structure—that is to say of intelligibility—in the thing. Matter is that which the form inheres in: in virtue of which the thing is an individual instance of the form which 'informs' it. But for Aristotle, as for Plato, it is axiomatic that the objects of knowledge are universal; hence, as for Plato, it is the forms of things which enter the mind in its knowing. This is true, for Aristotle, at every level of knowledge. In sensation, for instance, in hearing, a vibration set up in the air by a rhythmically vibrating body, affects the ear, which picks up the vibration and reproduces the rhythm in the sensitive organism. Hearing is simply such a reception in the sentient organism of an external rhythm. Rhythm for the Greeks is a prime example of form—we have already noticed how fascinated they were by the discovery that the pitch of sound could be mathe-matically correlated with the rhythm of a vibration. The case of hearing provides a clear instance of the form of an external sound being produced in the percipient without the matter in which it inhered. This is perhaps the clearest instance; but for Aristotle it justified the extension of this account to all sense-perception in general.

But sound, colour and so on are not the sum-total of the forms which define a thing; they are only its sensible forms. And sense-perception is not the whole of our knowledge of the world, even if it is the beginning and source of it all. To complete our very rudimentary picture of Aristotle's theory of knowledge, we must recall his view of the soul in the human composite.[1] The soul, for Aristotle, is one side of the living composite being; its correlative is the body. The soul is related to the body as form is to matter, and neither can exist without the other. The soul is what makes the difference between a living thing, plants, animals and men, and inanimate matter. It is a general term for all vital functions, on which the higher psychical functions may or may not be imposed, according to the kind of living being we are dealing with. In man, of course, we must allow scope for his characteristic form of activity, that of rational or intellectual knowledge. To oversimplify even more grossly than I have done hitherto: for Aristotle, rational knowledge in the mind is accounted for along the same lines as we have already seen in his account of sense-perception. The form—the intelligible form this time—is abstracted by the mind from the concrete individual just as its perceptible

[1] cp. above, p. 56.

form enters the sense-organ. Here, the intelligible form is impressed on the mind, without the individual matter, of course. Aristotle speaks of two parts, or perhaps of two aspects of mind: the receptive mind, which receives the intelligible form, and the active mind, which disengages the form from the individual concrete matter of the object and impresses it on the mind.

What Aristotle is denying in this account of knowledge is the doctrine of reminiscence, which we have seen Plato adopting from the Pythagoreans. For Aristotle, the mind has no *independent* access to knowledge, no knowledge brought with it from beyond this world; it can only receive what it knows from experiencing the world around it, through the body with which it forms one individual substance. He is not, of course, denying that the mind is active in its knowing; that is why he stresses so much the function of the active intellect. Its work is needed for making the latent intelligibility of things actual in the mind. It is the light which illuminates the objects of knowledge, just as visible light illuminates material objects and renders them visible. This is still the old analogy of the sun, now no longer outside the mind illuminating a world of forms, as for Plato, nor identified with God dwelling in the mind, but with the active role of the mind in understanding.

This was the theory of knowledge which St. Thomas Aquinas adopted along with the rest of the Aristotelian philosophy. Indeed I should say that it was perhaps the kernel of the serious philosophic thinking that appealed to him most of all in Aristotle's work. His own account is a refined version, following Aristotle's in all its essentials. He settles some of the controversial points arising from ambiguities left in Aristotle's account. He firmly rejects the view held at various times by commentators on Aristotle—and possibly by Aristotle himself—that the active mind does not strictly speaking belong to the individual human soul, but enters it from outside; identified, as it had sometimes been, with the mind of God. St. Thomas, while he certainly asserts —as Aristotle had also asserted—that the active mind can survive, though in an impoverished and imperfect state, after the death of the body, firmly rejects all such views. For St. Thomas the active mind is certainly part of the individual soul; this is to say that the work of understanding really is human work, not God acting in the mind: except, of course, in the sense in which God acts in everything.

Aquinas then took over the Aristotelian account of our way of knowing in its entirety. This is not to say that his theory of knowledge is not also intensely original: but its originality appears in the subtle elaboration of detail within the Aristotelian framework. I cannot go into this theory of knowledge in detail: to do so would take us too far afield. There is perhaps just one point which I ought to mention however, because it seems to be so enormously important in St. Thomas's own eyes: this is the central role he gives to what he calls the *phantasma* in the process of understanding. He may well have derived this notion from Aristotle along with the rest—but I am sure that his insistence on the key-position it holds in knowledge is something quite new. What exactly he means by a *phantasma* need not concern us here: it is, at any rate, a physical image derived from sense-perception, or something like it. What Aquinas insists on again and again is that without such a *phantasma* there is no knowledge. He is asserting two things in saying this: first, that sense-perception is, for human beings, in the last resort the source of all our knowledge; but he is also saying more than this. He is insisting on something that modern philosophers have come increasingly to recognize: that the mind is, in all its workings, closely dependent on manipulating symbols of some kind—words, mental pictures, whatever it may be—that there is not first a thought which is then embodied in words, but that in fact we cannot think except in terms of words, or something like them. Our thought is just seeing the symbol we use as significant. Its role is to endow the material furnished by experience with meaning. St. Thomas here has recourse to the hallowed analogy of light which renders the colours of things visible. Thought, in like manner, renders the data of experience meaningful; but there is no meaning without a vehicle for meaning. Whether you call this vehicle a *phantasma*, an image or a symbol, matters little.

St. Thomas's recourse to the light-analogy is a final reminder that he stands in the centre of the whole Greek tradition, which we have traced in Christian as well as classical Greek thought. It is true that in choosing to follow Aristotle he rejects Plato; but it is fascinating as well as instructive to see how he attempts to make his own the Platonism of St. Augustine. The reason why he rejects Plato is, of course, that the whole metaphysical picture of the separated forms and a knowledge of them deriving not from sense, but from reminiscence, is unacceptable to him. Augustine, as he was well aware, was basically a Platonist: what he did to the Platonic scheme, was according to St. Thomas's summary of his position, first, to put the forms inside the mind of God; and, secondly, to account for our knowledge in terms of our minds being illuminated by the divine light, instead of invoking, as Plato had done, an innate familiarity with the forms derived from another life. But in the Aristotelian scheme the forms are inherent in the physical things themselves; these yield their intelligibility to the mind under the mind's own illumination: here it is the active intellect that plays the role of the light. This is the way Aquinas chooses to follow: but he will go so far with Augustine as to say that the mind has recourse to divine illumination in order to understand or that the mind understands in virtue of being a created likeness of the divine light. The second way of talking, St. Thomas's, is much more uncompromisingly insistent on the fact that it is in the human mind that one must find all the factors that explain its working, even though one goes on to say that this mind itself is a kind of reflection of the divine mind. In so doing one has put what Augustine spoke of as divine activity in the mind's knowing, right inside the mind, and one has thereby made quite a new picture of it, and of its functioning. But what St. Thomas means to insist on when he assimilates St. Augustine's teaching to his own is that fundamentally, when all is said and done about the mechanism of our human knowing, he stands in the same Christian universe as Augustine; that the vision of its out-line and basic structure, all its being and functioning intimately dependent on its source and the goal of its striving, is still the same.[1]

[1]cp. E. Gilson, 'Pourquoi saint Thomas a critiqué saint Augustin', in *Arch. d'hist. doctr. & litt. du M.A.*, 1 (1926), pp. 5–127.

7

Love and the Will

IN our discussion of Greek and Christian views on the subject of knowledge, what we found was neither a contrast nor a convergence. Here, Christianity did not bring any specifically new view or doctrine with it; consequently, Christian thinkers felt themselves free to exploit the whole range of Greek thought when they came to formulate their own philosophical understanding of mind and mental activity. We traced two of the fundamental, divergent ways, utilizing two different Greek conceptions, along which Christian thought developed on this topic. Christianity, as such, remained, as it always must remain, fundamentally neutral between these two different philosophical views. Now when we come to talk about love, the situation is very different. Here Christianity did come into the field with a very definite, indeed quite a unique view of love, which, as we shall see, was radically different from all the Greek notions of love. In spite of the divergence of Greek and Christian views, however, a good many of the greatest Christian thinkers felt themselves able to draw on the Greek theories and to utilize them in the course of their exposition of the Christian view. How they did this, I shall try to show. Some theologians have thought that in doing so they

78

allowed the purity of the Gospel understanding of love to be corrupted, or even betrayed, by yielding to the seduction of Greek notions.[1]

This charge seems to me to arise from a mistaken view of the nature of theological thinking, and to over-simplify the opposition between the Greek and Biblical concepts. At any rate, what is unquestionable is that Christians did draw on Greek thought to a considerable extent in their attempts to gain intellectual insight into the love revealed in the New Testament. I shall start by surveying briefly what is specifically Christian, that is to say the Biblical understanding of love, then point out the contrast between this and previous Greek reflection, and finally I shall go on to show how Greek reflection came to be utilized in expounding the Christian view, by some of the outstanding Christian thinkers.

The word used in the New Testament which we translate by 'love' or by 'charity' is *agape*. It is noteworthy that this word is little used in classical Greek, and has no religious or philosophical importance. This, together with the fact that it had been used a great deal in the Greek translation of the Old Testament, may well account for the preference of the New Testament writers in choosing it rather than other Greek words which we also translate by 'love'. It is unnecessary to dwell on an idea as familiar as the New Testament idea of love, beyond spotlighting one or two characteristic marks from the point of view we shall be taking. What the New Testament has in mind when it speaks of love, is, of course, above all, God's love for men, manifested in the saving work of his Son, Jesus Christ. 'God so loved the world that he gave his own Son' (Jo. 3. 16) these words of the Fourth Gospel give perhaps the clearest

[1] See A. Nygren, *Agape and Eros*, E.tr. (London, 1953).

expression to what 'love' means in the New Testament. It is, then, first, God's love for men; and when St. John goes on to talk about men's love for God, and for one another, he makes it clear that he is still speaking of the same kind of love, even of the very same love: 'In this is love,' he says, 'not that we loved God but that he loved us' (I Jo. 4. 10); 'We love because he first loved us' (*ibid.*, 19). And the love enjoined upon men in the double commandment to love God and one's neighbour as oneself is one and the same love: it is to be a sharing in the divine love for men revealed and imparted in Christ.[1]

So much for the Biblical picture; now let us quickly enumerate some of the salient features of this love: it is first of all, a movement from God towards man, a sacrificial giving. It is completely unselfish ('it seeketh not its own'), but gratuitous and generous; it is freely bestowed on its object, irrespective of its value, or merits; indeed, one might go so far as to say that it creates value in its object. These are some of the most characteristic features of *agape*; what about the Greek conceptions of love?

The word *agape* is almost completely absent from Greek philosophy,[2] infrequent in literature, and when it does occur, is very colourless compared with the New Testament's usage. Whether the notion for which it stands is equally absent, we shall have to judge when we have discussed the nature of love as understood by the Greeks. We shall be concerned with two ideas, that of *eros* and that of

[1] On the Biblical conception(s) of love, see Kittel, *TWNT*, s.v. ἀγαπάω. (E. tr.: *Bible key-words: Love*, by G. Quell and E. Stauffer, London, 1949).

[2] See C. Spicq, 'Le verbe ἀγαπάω et ses dérivés dans le grec classique', in *Rev. Bibl.*, 60 (1953), pp. 372–97. I have not, at the time of writing, been able to consult Père Spicq's recent studies of Hellenistic and Biblical usages of the word.

philia—both of which we render by the word 'love', though
philia is often also translated by 'friendship'. Taking *eros*
first, then, we can do no better than to see what Plato has
to say about it. Our task is made unusually easy, because
Plato has put most of what he has to say on this together in
his dialogue the *Symposium*. I will not give a detailed summary of this exciting work here, but only lift out the
essentials in so far as they concern us.[1]

The first and most fundamental thing to be said about
eros as it appears in this work, is that it is *natural*. By this I
mean that *eros* belongs to a thing's nature just as much as do
others of its essential characteristics. It is that in each thing
or person—I want to stress that we are not concerned just
with human nature, but with things in general—which
determines the way in which the thing is inclined toward
other things; that is to say, it is the principle of all its
natural attractions and repulsions, in the case of animate
things also of their natural instincts and impulses. In the
most general terms *eros* is a cosmic principle of orientation,
the source and impulse to movement and activity. Aristotle
wove this idea into his physics in a universalized form: the
natural inclination which causes heavy things to fall, light
things to rise, animals to pursue their food and human
beings their desires and impulses is, at bottom, the same:
the orientation of each thing's nature to that which, by
nature, belongs to it. His divinity, being perfect in itself and

[1]For a more detailed discussion of this topic, see my paper 'The
dialectic of *eros* in Plato's Symposium', in *Downside Rev.*, 73
(1955), pp. 219–30. My thanks are due to the Editor for allowing
me to make use here of some of the material contained in this
article. cp. also F. M. Cornford, 'The doctrine of ἔρως in Plato's
Symposium' in *The Unwritten philosophy and other essays* (Cambridge,
1950); A. J. Festugière, *Contemplation et vie contemplative selon Platon*
(Paris, 1946), pp. 334ff., and *L'Enfant d'Agrigente* (Paris, 1941),
pp. 121ff.

having nothing lacking to itself, being static and devoid of movement, has no *eros* for anything outside itself: it is, however, the *object* of desire to less perfect things: 'it moves by being loved' (*Met.* Λ, 1072b4). Dante gives the most eloquent expression to this picture of the world:

> In the order I speak of all natures have their bent, according to their different lots, nearer to their source and farther from it; they move, therefore, to different ports over the great sea of being, each with an instinct given it to bear it on: this bears fire up towards the moon,—this is the motive force in mortal creatures,— this binds the earth together and makes it one. And not only the creatures that are without intelligence does this bow shoot, but those also that have intellect and love (*Parad.* 1.104–20).

Dante here gives generalized expression to the same notion of *eros* which Plato is describing in the *Symposium*.

What Plato is interested in particularly in the *Symposium* is this cosmic force as it manifests itself in human nature and activity. The first approach to the core of his view is contained in the speech he puts into the mouth of Aristophanes. This takes the form of a myth to account for the origin of human love. To summarize this profound joke is inevitably to do it grave injustice, but even at the cost of travesty, its relevance must be sketched in. Men were originally round, with two pairs of hands and legs, and everything duplicated. They were complete in themselves and had no need of a partner; it was only when their strength became a menace to the gods that Zeus cut them in half and Apollo patched them up and rearranged them and thus gave rise to the human race as we know it. The love which makes each person seek his or her partner is the radical insufficiency of their new, incomplete natures: it is the 'desire and pursuit of the whole'. *Eros* appears very clearly here as longing for union with an object perhaps only dimly known. Love is identified with this desire for self-completion by the loved object; the object is indeed defined simply as being the 'complement' of the lover's need. Plato, unlike many others who see love as essentially a matter of impulse, passion and desire, is ready to face up to the consequences of such a view. If love is conceived as the result of an essential incompleteness, or insufficiency in the lover, it is identical with the quest and desire of the loved object which is the complement of his lack. Love necessarily has an object, it is 'love of . . .'; but 'love of . . .' necessarily involves 'desire for . . .', and 'desire for . . .' is incompatible with 'possession of. . . '. In other words, once the lover obtains the satisfaction of his quest, once his need is met and his incompleteness filled up, love must, on such a view, cease. Plato saw this very clearly, and faced the dilemma which at this point presents itself: either perfect happiness—which is the fulfilment of all desire—cannot be attained; or love must cease on its being attained, since it must, by definition, involve unsatisfied desire.

There is no escape between the horns of this dilemma, short of re-defining 'love' in a way which loosens its logical connexion with 'unsatisfied desire'. That would, however, mean abandoning the basic category of *eros* as generally understood. Before considering how Plato solved this problem, it is as well to summarize the salient features of love understood in terms of *eros*. It would, first of all, be a grave mistake to think of *eros* as a matter of physical passion or sensual love. Sensual love, it is true, is *eros*; but the soul has its desire no less than the body, and no one insists more on the difference between the 'heavenly' *eros* and the 'vulgar' or sensual *eros* than does Plato. On the contrary, *eros*, for Plato provides the soul with the wings needed for its ascent from the beauty of material things to that of spiritual things, until it ultimately comes to rest where alone it can find its complete and final satisfaction, in the contemplation of the absolutely Beautiful itself. If then, we cannot contrast this view of love with the *agape* of the Bible by saying that it is sensual, whereas that is spiritual, where does the contrast lie?

Eros is desire and longing for its object: it is essentially acquisitive, not giving. It is embedded in the nature of the lover, in his radical insufficiency and need; this manifests itself as desire, passion—impulsive love, not deliberately chosen, not capable of being commanded. It is essentially self-centred: the loved object is desired as 'that which would meet *my* need, fulfil *my* desire'. And in relation to God, it is applicable only—as Aristotle realized—to man's love of God: his desire to rest in the contemplation of God's eternal perfection. God, being perfect, cannot love, in this sense of love. He can only be the object of desire, but cannot himself desire anything.

This *eros* is at the opposite pole from the *agape* which we have seen is the distinctive love of the Bible. In these terms, obviously, the love of which the Bible speaks cannot be understood; the two things are diametrically opposed and have nothing in common except their name—and not even that in Greek. It is tempting to say that Christian thinkers ought simply to have noted the two different things we call 'love' and confined each to its proper sphere: *eros* to the sphere of nature—inanimate, living and human, *agape* to God's love, and man's in so far as it was like it.

This, however, is just the point at which the difficulty arises; if *agape* is at all applicable to human love of any

kind, how is it related to the universal type of love extending throughout the realm of nature, including that of men,
to the love we know as *eros*, which seems, on the face of it,
to be such a very different thing? What is there in human
nature for the divine initiative in *agape* to grasp?

A simple answer would have been 'nothing'. The love
enjoined upon us in the divine commandment would not
then be human in any sense whatsoever. It would simply
be God's love flowing through us, but not even taking us
with it, merely using humanity as a vehicle, a pipe-line.
Our genuinely human activity could not be brought into
any kind of relation with it—it would remain where it was
without it. Indeed, it is difficult to see how man could be
commanded to love in this way, if this kind of love were in
no sense a human activity. Another answer would have been
to give a different kind of account of human love; after all,
there is no reason why the *eros*-account should have been
accepted by the early Christian thinkers to the exclusion of
any other.

They might for instance, have abandoned all Greek
thought about *eros* and drawn on the other stream of Greek
reflection on love, that on *philia*. This word had none of the
philosophical overtones of *eros*. It means affection in a
general sense: rather more than our word 'friendship'—
though it does include that—as it includes family love. But
as Aristotle suggests, it is a purely ethical concept, and
irrelevant to reflection on the actual *nature* of men (*Eth.
Nic.*, VIII.1155b7–12). I suggest that why *philia* was never
to play more than a subsidiary role in Christian thinking
about love is just this fact; it offered valuable insight into
human relationships, but none into the nature on which
these are built. The concern of Christian thinkers with *eros*,
in spite of its *prima facie* difficulty of being pressed into

service, is a concern with human nature—and with nature in general. In the Greek theory of *eros*, Christian thinkers found a conceptual structure in terms of which human nature could be understood as part of an overall cosmic pattern. This is why they accepted it, in broad outline, at least; but the form in which they did accept it was much more elastic, wider and at the same time more profound, than the form in which I have hitherto presented it. To a very large extent, it is true, it was their own work that so widened and deepened the conception of *eros* as to make it a fit instrument of *agape*; but to some extent they could find the direction of their own work anticipated by Plato and Aristotle, and other Greek thinkers.

A break with the simple view of *eros* which I have so far been describing is hinted at by Plato in the *Symposium*. The point at which we left Plato was that at which we found him confronting the dilemma: perfect happiness consists in perfect possession of the object of desire, the fulfilment of all desire; but *eros* by definition, involves desire. Hence either perfect happiness is unattainable, or love must cease on its being attained. The manner in which Plato solves this problem is the only way in which one can go about solving it if one wants to say that perfect happiness is compatible with enduring love: that is, by loosening the connexion of love with unsatisfied desire. He does this in a remarkably unobtrusive way, so unobtrusive that it has often escaped notice altogether. He goes on to describe the soul's journey, borne on the wings of *eros* from love of particular beautiful things on to love of beautiful things in general, and from love of material beauty to love of universal and spiritual beauty. The whole tone of this discussion, by the way, is very reminiscent of the language of Greek mystery religion: we are given to understand that the journey of *eros* is a purification, a preparation for the disclosure of the divine vision. At the end of its gradual ascent through dim and fragmentary intimations the soul is united with the perfect archetypal Beauty in a blaze of light wherein it beholds the ultimately real.

All this is still sound *eros*-doctrine; but there is an important hint Plato throws out in the course of it, which is less so. This hint is given when Plato is about to give a completely general definition of *eros*. He defines *eros* now as 'desire for perpetual possession of the good'. (206B). What is more important here than the stress on the qualifying adjective 'perpetual', is the new meaning he gives to 'good'. Hitherto the good had simply been identical with that which satisfies desire; that is to say, that in each particular thing in virtue of which it is desired. But notice that desire for 'the good' is not like desire for money, or for physical prowess, or for sexual satisfaction, or even for knowledge, only differing from desires like these in having 'the good' for its object. It differs from all these desires in being desire in a very different sense. Plato insists on this forcibly when he alludes to the myth about *eros* which had been propounded earlier in the dialogue, with a staggering discrimination which in effect marks a complete change of perspective. This is how he makes Diotima (the prophetess who is instructing Socrates) allude to the view put forward by Aristophanes earlier in the dialogue: 'There is indeed a theory that lovers are people in search of the other half of themselves; but according to my view of the matter, love is not desire either of the half or the whole, unless that half or whole happens to be good' (205E). 'Good', that is to say, is no longer just that which satisfies desire; and love is no longer the whole complex of passions, desires and impulses which direct all activity: it is also directive of these passions,

C.F.—G

desires and impulses themselves. Love is now not only subject to ethical criteria for its assessment, but at the same
time provides these criteria and performs the activity of
assessment.

Plato, while adhering to his basic notion that *eros* is the
directive principle of all activity, here passes well beyond
the limits of the original conception of *eros* as we found it
expressed, for instance, by Aristophanes in his speech. That
picture of love—love as an incompleteness seeking completion by its complement—is now, to all intents and purposes, abandoned. Plato now turns to a quite different
desire as being the essence of love, the desire for procreation.
And this is desire of a very different kind: it is the desire of
a being already complete to overflowing; this desire cannot
be thought of as a lack; it is not for something to be ob-
tained, but for giving forth from oneself. All this is worked
out with a subtle dramatic appropriateness in the *Symposium*; but we must pass on to a consideration of how
Christian thinkers opened widely the door that Plato had
just managed to set ajar.

For obvious reasons, there was a good deal in the
Platonic theory of *eros*, particularly in the form given it by
later Platonists like Plotinus, by which it would commend
itself very strongly to a Christian mind. The picture of a
world coming forth from God by way of a procession of
forms, in their orderly hierarchy, only needed a modicum
of reinterpretation to fit the Christian doctrine of creation.
In the Platonic account this world was animated through
and through by the upward aspiration towards its origin,
which was also the goal of all its movement and activity,
its last end. Man's place in this world fits into this 'great
chain of being'. The soul, exiled from its real home by being
embodied, need only turn from the relative worthlessness

of material things to the pursuit of its real goal, the pursuit of the primal Beauty and Goodness. Animated by this desire it ascends through the stages of its original descent until it comes to rest again in an ecstatic union with God. It is a tempting picture for a Christian to swallow wholesale: not only because it gives so sublime an account of the whole cosmos, but also because it appears to provide for all that a Christian would want as a guide to living: it stresses that *ascesis* of will and mind in which it is only too easy to recognize the evangelical warning that only the pure in heart shall see God. This could very easily be transformed into a Christian account of the world and of human salvation by simply making the return to God conditional on the help of Christ's saving work.

It is a tempting picture, and some of the earliest Christian thinkers fell for it. Origen, for instance, seemed so captivated by it that he seems at times quite oblivious to the *agape* which is revealed in Christ. He will, for instance, commit himself to the staggering claim that those who are well versed in the ways of the Scriptures and have attained to a deep spiritual insight into their meaning, are to understand whatever it says about *agape* as if it were said about *eros*, 'caring nothing about words'. For the two things are the same, Origen says; only the Scriptures prefer to use the more 'respectable' word lest they mislead the weaker brethren by appearing to commend carnal desire and passion. Origen is so completely in the grip of his Platonist outlook at this point, that he never asks himself whether there can be any real difference between the two things. He is so uncritical of the validity of his Platonic pre-suppositions that he is misled in his reading of a phrase of St. Ignatius of Antioch who had said 'My *eros* is crucified'—meaning thereby that his carnal lusts and passions had been crucified and that he is now risen to new life in Christ.[1] But Origen misunderstands this, and takes it to mean '(Christ), my love, is crucified' and infers that it is legitimate to call God *eros*, just as the Fourth Gospel calls him *agape*. (*Comm. in Cant., Prol.*)

Now even though it be true that Origen's fully worked-out teaching on charity is very close to an authentically Biblical perspective, although the Neoplatonic doctrine of *eros* plays a considerable part in its formulation, it is clear that misunderstandings such as this are both significant and dangerous. For even if it is legitimate for a Christian theologian to go to work on the Biblical revelation with philosophical equipment; and even if the conception of *eros* in this equipment is the more subtle and transformed conception of *eros* as delight in good perpetually possessed and leading to spontaneous giving-out, ought not the theologian's work to start from the keenest possible awareness of the uniqueness of the revealed love of the New Testament? Are we not perilously near to thinking of the evangelist's statement as a philosophically unsophisticated version of Platonism? At this point Origen, though surely one of the greatest of theologians, has allowed himself to be led astray by a too uncritical acceptance of Platonic modes of thought and expression. Similar statements can be found in the writings of later theologians of a Platonic cast of mind, for instance in the works of the pseudo-Areopagite. Instead of pursuing further examples of such statements, however, let us turn to an even greater—and less uncritical

[1]On this still debated passage and Origen's interpretation of it, see A. von Harnack, 'Der "Eros" in der alten christlichen Literatur', in *S.B. preuss. Akad. Wiss.*, 1918, pp. 81–94; C. Bigg, *The Christian Platonists of Alexandria* (Oxford, 1913), pp. 6–9; and F. J. Dölger, 'Christus als himmlischer Eros und Seelenbräutigam bei Origenes' in *Antike und Christentum*, 6 (1950), pp. 273–5.

—Christian Platonist, Augustine, to see how he incorporates the Platonic view of love into a Christian vision.

Augustine, of course, wrote in Latin; and whatever may have been the original Latin usage, by Augustine's time the Latin terminology of love was fairly blurred; and although Latin had at least three words normally used to mean love— *amor, dilectio,* and *caritas*—it had almost as little means of rendering the contrast between *eros* and *agape* as has English with its single word 'love'.[1] Augustine's language, therefore, gives us very little clue as to where he stands in relation to the opposition of *eros* and *agape*. To see where he stands, we must trace similarities of theme and treatment; and these are striking indeed. He is writing very much within the framework of the Platonic-Aristotelian tradition when he represents love as analogous to weight:

> 'Bodies,' he writes in a famous passage, 'tend by their weight to move towards the place proper to them. . . . Fire tends upwards, stone downwards . . . moved by their weight, they seek their proper place. Things out of place are not at rest; they come to rest in being brought to their right place. *My* weight is my love: wherever I am carried, it is by it that I am carried' (*eo feror quocumque feror*—*Conf.* XIII. 9.10).

Man's proper place is in the presence of God—it is towards God that the inclination implanted in man is turned, whether he knows this or not; we recall the equally famous exclamation at the very beginning of the *Confessions*: 'Thou O God hast made us for thyself, and our hearts are restless till they rest in Thee' (*Conf.* I.1.1). So far there is nothing new here, except of course, the echo of St. Augustine's own

[1] cp. H. Pétré, *Caritas: Étude sur le vocabulaire latin de la charité chrétienne* (Louvain, 1948).

spiritual struggle. It may well be that his transformation of the philosophical picture he inherited must also be traced back to this struggle.[1]

The notion of a struggle, a conflict, or a tension to be resolved, is indeed, central to Augustine's understanding of love. He knew only too well that although man's whole natural orientation is godward, he can, if he so chooses, refuse to follow his 'natural bent', if we may speak in such terms. He could follow other inclinations—other loves—which need not pull the same way. Augustine had experienced their power; the duality of love of which he so often speaks was something he had felt on his own pulse. Man is a being compounded of flesh and spirit, a being, furthermore, deprived by sin of its original integrity. Rival loves, conflicting impulses and diverging desires are his inescapable lot. Here Augustine simplifies a little, reducing the multifarious impulses in man to two loves: *cupiditas*, the perverse love which drags man down, and *caritas*, the authentic human love which lifts man up towards his real, spiritual home. Somewhere he describes the human task as being a 'transference of weight' from *cupiditas* to *caritas* (*Ep.* 157.9).

This, still, is not really radically new: it is still the Greek notion of the vulgar and the heavenly *eros*, revitalized in terms of Christian experience. I have just mentioned Augustine's analogy of a transference of weight: I should like to underline this notion, because I am sure that it is in scrutinizing this that the novelty of his view of love appears best. This shifting of weight, that is to say the choice between the two loves—is itself, to his mind, a work of love. There is a more fundamental duality of love than the

[1]On Augustine's teaching about love, see J. Burnaby, *Amor Dei* (London, 1938).

duality between *cupiditas* and *caritas*; there is, in addition, the love which chooses between the two, which decides, in the last resort, which is to prevail. Love, in other words, is natural inclination and impulse at the same time as it is self-imposed inclination, that is to say, deliberately chosen, duty. Love is involved in what a thing is, its nature, and determines its inclination towards other things. This is true of man just as it is of lower things; but man is the only creature who is not only what he was made to be, but also what he makes himself. His love, therefore, is what inclines him to seek not only what he was made to seek, but also what he makes himself seek. This curious duality—perhaps 'openness' would be a better word—had already, as I suggested, been glimpsed by Plato when he saw that the simple, one-level *eros*-theory just didn't explain human love. But it was Augustine who first made this duality about love central to his reflection. I shall have a good deal more to say in the next chapter about aspects of his thought which are pivoted on this notion.

What I have spoken of as the duality, or openness which is characteristic of human beings is explicitly recognized by St. Thomas Aquinas as the foundation of his theory of the human mind and will. It is important to appreciate that when I speak of such a duality, I do not mean to refer to the fact that the human composite is made up of body and mind; I am trying to draw attention to a character of the mind itself. Mind, or spirit, is by nature, according to Aquinas, different from all other natural things in being so to speak, on two levels at once. As we saw, in the previous chapter, in the process of knowing it is both active and receptive; this is brought out by his language which distinguishes between an active and a passive intellect, both of which have their work in understanding. Mind, then, alone of all created things, is unique in being not only what it is by nature, but in being able to make itself what it is not already. It is able to 'inform' itself, that is to say, to take on a diversity of forms or natures by its own spontaneous activity.

Now the Thomist theory of the will and of voluntary activity is a straightforward consequence of this view of the mind. Things in general have their fixed natures or forms, and consequently they have naturally determined inclinations towards other things to which they are related. The attainment of their natural aims is the achievement of their own perfection; all things always desire their own perfection, wherein they come to rest once it is attained. By 'desire', we must, of course, understand here the universal cosmic principle which the stone, for instance, displays when it 'desires' to fall to the place natural to it. Just as things in general have this desire or inclination which is the principle of their natural movement and function, so the mind has its desire or inclination. But since the nature of mind is what we described as 'open', that is to say that it can determine itself to an infinite variety of natures, so its desires or inclinations will reflect the infinite variety of forms the mind can impose on itself. Just as each natural thing has some particular, specific inclination in some particular direction, its own proper 'good', so the mind has an open, indeterminate inclination to good in general. In imposing particular forms upon itself, it imposes particular inclinations to particular goods. A stone, by nature, falls downwards if unsupported, being what it is; but man, in an important sense, makes himself. In virtue of having a mind, he can freely choose what to be, and therefore what to do and what to love. The spontaneity in human nature for imposing different inclinations on itself is what we call 'will'.

Love, in its most general sense, in the Thomist view is the *eros* we have described and seen to be running through Augustine as well as Plato: it is the dynamic aspect of each particular thing, the principle of its attractions to and repulsions from other things. For spiritual creatures, likewise, love is the dynamism of the mind's spontaneity. Here alone is love the infinitely varied thing it is, because man is the sort of creature who can make himself any of the infinitely varied sorts of being that are within his reach. The desires he can impose on himself are infinitely varied—indeed in speaking the language of *eros* and of desire, we must not blind ourselves to the fact that desires so imposed on oneself may be very far from 'desires' as normally understood; to follow them may, and often does, go very much against the grain. They may range from the wholly self-centred desire of passion to the wholly selfless sacrifice of the man who lays down his life for another.

So far I have spoken about human love very much as if men were simply mind and will. This is, of course, a grotesque parody, and in the next chapter we shall have to look a little more closely at the interplay of all the factors which go to the making of human action and conduct. To sum up the argument of this chapter, I shall conclude by suggesting what, as it seems to me, has happened to the *eros-agape* opposition in the course of the philosophical development of which I have tried to trace some of the more important stages. We began with a simple contrast of two opposed forms of love: the self-centred, passionate love of desire, *eros*, and the wholly selfless love revealed in the Gospel under the name of *agape*. We then looked more closely at the Platonic picture of *eros*, and found that it was, to say the least, only loosely related to the self-centred kind of love which goes by this name. We then saw this crack in the philosophy of *eros* widen—and in the end, the original, crude picture of the two opposed forms of love seems to have become completely transformed. *Eros*, instead of being the name of one of the two opposed types, has become the name for love in general. Love in general is understood on the analogy of the fundamental notions involved in the original meaning of *eros*, those of impulse, desire, inclination. But we have seen how very tenuous the relation becomes to the original, crude sense of words like 'desire' etc. as soon as one begins to speak of self-imposed desires and inclinations: so much so that the transformed *eros* is no longer contrasted with the selflessness of *agape*, but now includes this as one of the possible forms which *eros* is able to take. This kind of 'stretching' of language is, perhaps, a typical case of the procedure of metaphysical thinking. Whatever may be said about the metaphysics of love built on the analogy of *eros*, the charge that it obliterates the basic distinction between two opposed forms of love is one to which it is immune.

8

Reason and Conduct

WE discussed in the last chapter the philosophical accounts given by Plato, Aristotle, St. Augustine and St. Thomas of the basic springs of human action, that is to say, of their theories of the natural inclinations, of love and of the will. Now we must examine human action itself, from the point of view of its morality, that is to say in so far as it can be called good or bad, right or wrong. To do this adequately would take us very much beyond the limits of this chapter. In discussing this topic, then, I must be content to pick and choose even more haphazardly than elsewhere from the wealth of the relevant material. The choice is, inevitably, a personal one, and stresses a personal assessment of what is of overriding importance.[1]

It would be an undue oversimplification of the picture to suggest that the outstanding characteristic of Greek moral reflection, at any rate from Socrates onwards, is its concern to see human action and conduct as rational; any such generalization would be misleading—but this is the

[1]Since the completion of this chapter, J. Ferguson's stimulating book *Moral values in the ancient world* (London, 1958), has covered much of the ground not here dealt with. Its conclusions with regard to love are in some respects different from mine in Ch. 7.

97

strand in Greek ethical thought to which I shall confine my attention. In reading Plato's accounts of the anguished searching of Socrates for the definitions of moral concepts like courage, justice, temperance, and so forth, it is fatally easy to think of these as little more than a logical exercise, all very well for those with a questioning bent of mind, but really rather unnecessary for the ordinary man with a general sense of practical wisdom, expressing itself in actions consonant with common decency. But after all, Socrates was put to death for what his contemporaries thought he had been trying to do; and it is important for us to appreciate the challenge that his questionings had thrown down to them. The key to this, is perhaps, to be found in the hints in which Thucydides allows us to glimpse something of the moral corruption that was beginning to sweep across the whole Greek world. Athens herself, the chief glory of this world, had been affected: even for her, expediency had become the rule of conduct, and the most serious international crimes had been sanctioned in its name. And it was not a matter only of acting corruptly; like the rest of us, the Greeks were anxious to soothe their consciences, as Thucydides tells us. After speaking of the revolutions which had broken out in several Greek cities, the violence and subterfuge in the methods of seizing power and the atrocities committed in revenge, he goes on to comment on the ensuing corruption of the language of morals: 'The accustomed meanings of words, too, they changed at their will and pleasure to accord with their deeds. Thought-less recklessness was now reputed the courage of a party-member; provident caution was now cowardice under a fine name; moderation was now the pretext for unmanliness, and to seek to understand a question from all sides was to be incapable of acting' (III. 82). Thucydides' catalogue goes on, but this allows us to perceive the insidious corruption to which he is calling attention. Like George Orwell in our own day, he saw that when men's language about right and wrong is itself under attack, then moral decay has gone very far indeed: so far that unless an effort is made to 'purify the dialect of the tribe', all moral awareness is threatened.

With this in mind, it is easier to appreciate the point of simple questions of the kind that Socrates was fond of asking. In seeking the definitions of moral terms, he was expressing the overriding need to get our moral language right. In asserting the supremacy of law over power, of right over expediency and so on, he was recalling his fellow-Athenians to an older moral ideal which was beginning to get lost in the upheavals of the later fifth century. Plato no doubt went a good deal beyond the actual teaching of his master, Socrates: but his ethical concern, at any rate, stands in the same line. Right and wrong in action were not a matter of opinion, law is not simply what a ruling clique has the power to impose and to enforce. Law, right and wrong belong to the fabric of the world, they are to be discerned in it as objectively real; more real, indeed, for Plato, than the visible world of experience. For the moral forms, like the rest of them, are discerned by reason. Good action is, for Plato, an expression of rationality: his very definition of virtue as knowledge makes this clear, clear even to the point of over-emphasis. Whatever may be said in criticism of this over-intellectualistic formulation, it does insist on the specifically human type of excellence. 'Virtue', for a Greek, meant simply the specific excellence of each thing in relation to what it was meant to be and do. The virtue of a knife must be assessed in terms of its function, that of cutting. If it is to be good at this, its particular task, it must be sharp. Human excellence, likewise, consists in man being good at his own special function—which is the expression of rationality in all his being and all his activity.

Plato makes a number of separate approaches to this ideal of human excellence, starting from various individual virtues belonging to particular fields of action or types of men. But in the end, one gets the impression that all the special virtues merge in one inclusive definition, and that Plato is not really interested in their individual distinctive features, their differences from one another. This is something that Aristotle turned his attention to, without really departing from the fundamentals of Platonic ethics, as I have presented them. Following the more empirical direction of his interests, he paid more attention to the description of the individual virtues. He also revised the notion of 'virtue' as such, in a manner which I shall have to mention later on when we come to speak of Thomist ethics. There is another school of Greek philosophers to whose teaching I want briefly to refer before we pass on to Christian thought on this subject, the Stoic school.

The Stoic philosophers tried to express the same kind of concern as Plato's in terms of their own view of the world. For them, too, morality was rationality in action. The world, conceived in a fundamentally materialistic sense, was wholly determined by a law immanent in it which governed all processes and happenings. You could call the law in all things either 'natural' or 'divine': the two things came to the same, because Stoic pantheism in effect identified divinity with the whole system of the cosmos, conceived on the analogy of a great organism. Human action is not exempt from this law: it is fully determined by its necessity, just as other natural processes are. Man has no choice but to obey. He has a choice in the manner of his obedience only. The soul is, by nature, akin to the subtle attenuated fire which the Stoics called *pneuma*; this, they said, pervades the whole cosmos and is the principle of its life. Hence knowledge of the laws of natural process is natural to the soul—and it can willingly identify itself with the pervasive law, or rebel, but inevitably be frustrated in choosing rebellion. The Stoic ideal is that of identification with the natural law, in such a way that the course of human life in accordance with the necessity of law is accepted with detachment. The passions are a disturbance. They are not subject to reason and law, but are perversions of nature, so they have, not to be controlled, but to be eradicated. This completes the ideal of the Stoic ethics: that of a man willingly submissive to the law of nature, with no forces within him to pull him aside: the ideal of *apatheia*, of indifference to external environment.

The Stoic system was, in the long run, to prove unacceptable to Christian thinkers. Its materialism, and the thorough-going determinism so characteristic of it, did not lend themselves easily to utilization by Christian thinkers. Nevertheless, the idea of a law running through nature, and of the mind's affinity to it, made a lasting impression on Christian thought.[1] Echoes of it can be heard in the Middle Ages and later, in the theory of natural law.

When we turn to Christian reflection on action and conduct, we must, of course, bear in mind that the ideal of Christian excellence as well as the ordinary rules of Christian behaviour were *given*. That is to say, Christian thinkers did not, could not, begin with laying down an ideal—the ideal was there, in the New Testament, both in the example of the Lord as well as in his exhortation, and in St. Paul's moral teaching. These had authoritative claims

[1] cp. M. Spanneut, *Le stoïcisme des Pères de l'Église* (Paris, 1957), particularly pp. 231–69.

on the Christian community, and the anxious debate about what constitutes the good life which one finds, for instance, in Aristotle is, for Christians, a thing of the past. A great deal of moral perplexity does, of course, remain—but to define the aim of life as a whole is no longer the moralist's concern. He can, of course, bring the notions of Greek moral reflection to bear on his understanding of human destiny as revealed in the New Testament. And it is only fair to say that Christian theologians found in Greek thinking of the kind which I have outlined a very useful means of insight, and one which lent itself readily to being incorporated in a Christian vision of the world, of man and of God.

I want to by-pass the earlier stages of this assimilation of Greek thought in Christian moral theory, and to come straight to Augustine. This is not to say that previous Christian reflection is without interest, or even that it is without importance or lasting influence. But in Augustine— and Aquinas, with whom we shall be concerned after Augustine—we can, I think, see the insights of earlier reflection on this subject preserved, passed into the Christian tradition. If we were to deal anything like fully with this subject, this procedure would, of course, be quite indefensible. To give only two examples: the history of early Christian ethics would be grievously incomplete if the ethical teaching of St. Ambrose were omitted: his re-interpretation in a Christian setting of Ciceronian ethics, largely Stoic in inspiration, was certainly a very great achievement.[1] But through his brilliant convert, Augustine, much of what was of most lasting value in Ambrose's synthesis, passed into

[1] cp. T. Deman, 'Le *De Officiis* de saint Ambroise dans l'histoire de la théologie morale', in *Revue des sciences philosophiques et théologiques*, 37 (1953), pp. 409–24.

the generally accepted moral currency of Western Christendom. Again, the Platonism of some of the greatest of the Greek fathers is not sufficiently different, fundamentally, from Augustine's Platonism for us to pause in our course to discuss it. Reasons like these are my only excuse for leaving out such a very great deal both of interest and of importance.

We have already spoken about two aspects of St. Augustine's thought, his theory of knowledge and his theory of love. His ethics is the result of putting these two together. All knowledge, in his view, as we saw earlier, is ultimately the work of the divine light illuminating the mind. This goes for moral knowledge, knowledge of good and evil, of right and wrong, as much as for anything else: indeed, it would be fairer to say that moral judgement made in the light of the divine ideas is the model on which Augustine conceives all other types of judgement. This moral illumination reaches man through his conscience—which is not a separate faculty, but simply the mind considered as capable of making moral judgements under the illumination of the eternal truth. With regard to action, the eternal truth is eternal *law*. In so far as this enters our minds and supplies them with the ultimate rules of conduct, it is identical with the natural law: the natural law is simply that of the eternal which is accessible to the mind, just as the first principles of knowledge are that much of the eternal truth as the mind has access to under the illumination of the natural light. We are very close here to the Greek view of natural law: both views insist that law, the criterion of good and bad, belongs to the stuff of reality; that the mind, being by nature akin to the real, is capable of knowing it; and that we thus have an awareness of the unconditional claims being made upon us by a law which is above us and resists all our attempts to

C.F.—H

identify it with that which serves our interests, our pleasures, social expediency, or whatever it may be. It is simply there, one cannot get away from it, one must acknowledge its unconditional authority.

I have just said that the natural law—or eternal law, or moral law—it scarcely matters which one chooses to speak in terms of—that the law resists any attempt on our part to identify it with our interests or pleasures. Does that mean that it is callously indifferent to the fate of man, merely soliciting his obedience but promising nothing in return? There is, of course, an easy way out. This consists in saying that God rewards the just and punishes the unjust: but the greatest Christian thinkers have always seen that this *is* an easy way out, and not really a solution to the problem. Because after all, there is such a thing as wholly self-disregarding action, wholly selfless love: and if all one's action is in view of the promised reward or punishment, then whatever it is, it is certainly not selfless. But still, one could say that a beneficent Creator has so disposed of things that in obeying the moral law, one is, whether one knows it or not, in fact fulfilling one's own nature, and thereby doing what is ultimately conducive to its most complete satisfaction.

This suggestion brings us very much closer to the way in which St. Augustine, and St. Thomas, too, saw the question. But even now we must be careful not to misunderstand their position. When they insist that in fulfilling the demands of the moral law man is fulfilling his own nature, they mean first of all that man is rational, and that only behaviour in accordance with law is rational behaviour. They do not mean that acting in accordance with law is a kind of long-term insurance policy. They know very well that fully human, that is to say fully rational action, can be a very costly business. Their concern is first of all to insist on man's need to recognize the unconditional authority of law, because only in so doing does he express his nature, that of rationality. The ultimate consequences of his actions—including his reward—must be left to the mercy of God; it still remains for man, when he has done all, to admit that he is an unprofitable servant.

I have been speaking of 'law'; and I am aware that this word may be misleading. It is easier to say what is not meant by the word when we use it in this context than what is. It does not mean a lengthy, complex code of commands and prohibitions, like the legislation of a state, or even the individually propounded divine commandments found in the Bible. It means simply what, in any case in which we are faced with alternative ways of acting, manifests itself as what we *ought* to do, that which we must acknowledge as binding upon our allegiance. Individual, propounded laws are abstract, general—they apply to types of cases. The moral law, natural, eternal law—call it what you will—extends to the concrete case, in all its uniqueness. It is not a question, when one is in real moral perplexity, of reminding oneself of a general, abstract law, and trying to apply it to one's particular case; no, it is a matter of discerning the validity of an unconditional demand impinging on one in this, particular, concrete case.

Rationality, then, displays itself in human action in so far as this is submitted to the demands of law. Such a statement may seem surprising in view of Augustine's famous and oft-repeated saying: 'Love, and do what you will' (*In Ep. Joann. Tr.* VII. 8). The emphasis here seems to be on freedom rather than on law, on love rather than on reason —just the contrary of what I have been suggesting. Is there really an opposition here, or even a divergence of emphasis?

To answer this question, I should like to begin with a reminder of what was said in the last chapter about love. We noticed a peculiar duality in human love, a duality in virtue of which man has not only the natural desires and inclinations implanted in him, but also those which he freely imposes upon himself. This is part of the peculiar nature of rational or spiritual creatures. Such creatures, man among them, are, in a certain sense, self-creative: mind is the openness which can spontaneously 'make' itself. Man's natural inclinations all have their particular objects: his cravings for bodily sustenance, for sexual satisfaction, for social intercourse and so on; and they are all good—particular, determinate goods. But the mind is inclined to good in general; in its self-creative spontaneity it chooses among individual goods, and gives itself particular inclinations to the particular objects of its free choice. The demands of law, or reason, are the demand that the mind follow in its self-creation the exigencies of rationality. In following these, both love and the action in which it issues will express the order of reason. How little law and love are capable of being opposed, in Augustine's view, is most clearly shown by his definition of virtue as the 'order of love' (*de Civ. Dei*, XV. 22). Love, imposing on itself the order demanded of it, becomes 'ordered love'—in all its inclinations and works following the moral law. If one acts from love like this, one can indeed do what one will; love like this has made the law its own, it freely and spontaneously enacts its commandments. It should, of course, be added, that for Augustine, love is always only painfully ordered, and piecemeal, imperfectly; to be really wholly possessed by it, so that one spontaneously and consistently acts from a rightly ordered love, is a gift of grace, present only in the perfection of charity and holiness.

For most of us, however, the achievement of virtue, of an 'ordered love', as Augustine has defined it, is a matter of unending struggle, of tension and striving. The good that we will we do not, but the evil we will not, that we do; we are only too painfully aware of another law in our members at war with the law we recognize as claiming our allegiance. What we come up against, at this point, is the insufficiency of the over-simplified account I have so far given of love. For all the time, in speaking of the mind's inclination to good, and its self-imposed inclination, that is to say its capacity to recognize duty, I have left out of account the fact that men are not minds, but flesh and blood. They are composite beings; and if we follow Augustine, we must go on to say even that there is an element of distortion in their nature, a loss of the sort of integrity which would guarantee that the different elements which go to the making of this nature always work together for good. We need not discuss the theological reasons in terms of which Augustine explained this fact. I do not think that we need look far into ourselves to realize, at any rate, that it is a fact—and this is enough for our present purpose.

Human action is always and inevitably set in the context of the pulls and pressures of different impulses, desires, fears and hopes. It is in their midst that rationality has to be expressed by moral action. So far we have spoken of the mind recognizing the law, forming itself in accordance with it and thereby 'ordering' its love. What does this mean in relation to our particular desires, say for the satisfaction of our bodily needs, our social aspirations, even say, our intellectual curiosities? All these are so many individual desires for individual goods; and as the selection I have just given suggests, they are a mixed bag, some of them purely physical, some purely intellectual, and a good many involving both our physical and our spiritual natures. The point about them all is that they are particular inclinations towards particular objects. In ordering itself according to reason or law, the mind is in fact choosing among these. It is always having to discard the pursuit of some good for that of another, to renounce the unlawful for the lawful, the lesser for the greater. For Augustine, the subject of moral assessment is the will itself, not the individual impulses with which it identifies itself or from which it dissociates itself. One cannot say about the lust or the greed which tempts one that it is morally evil, unless one does in fact choose to follow their impulses in opposition to one's plain duty or the dictates of a rightly ordered love. What one judges is the will which identifies itself with them at the cost of renouncing what it knows it ought to choose.

> 'An upright will,' Augustine says, 'is good love, a perverse will is bad love. Love as longing for what it loves is desire; as possessing and enjoying it, it is joy; flying what it hates, it is fear; feeling its presence it is pain; all these are evil, if the love is evil, good if it be good' (*de Civ. Dei*, XIV. 7.2).

We have now filled in some of the content of the empty outline formula we began with, according to which virtue was defined as the 'order of love'. The order which is here envisaged is necessarily an order of law manifested among the manifold and perplexing impulses of human living.

The order of love then, to use a slightly paradoxical formula which nevertheless, I hope, conveys some meaning as a result of what I have said about love, is love imposing order on manifold loves. Virtue consists in willing what we should will, loving what we ought to love. What relevance has this definition, on the one hand, to our moral judgements of persons, and to their individual actions, on the other? When we talk about virtue in this general way, what are we to make of particular virtues, like courage, temperance, prudence and so on? And what about, say, the coward, who, by an exceptional heroic effort manages to perform one brave action and then relapses into his habitual cowardice: are we to call him a courageous man? Or are we to say that at that moment and that moment only, he was a courageous man? Or that, though a coward, he acted like a brave man? All these are questions—or different sides of the same question, as we shall see—in which Augustine is not interested. They bring us to Aquinas, once again, who here, perhaps even more than elsewhere, is very much a follower of Augustine: but as always, he brings something new for which he manages to find a place within Augustine's teaching—and this element of novelty, in this case, as so often, is something he learnt from Aristotle. What we are going to look at to round off this discussion of rationality in human conduct is the fundamentally Aristotelian theory of virtue as it appears in Aquinas.

We may start by observing the interesting comment that Aquinas makes on the definition of virtue as the 'order of love'. This he accepts, but with a refinement. Virtue is the 'order of love', he says, in the sense that 'ordered love' is the object of all virtue; for in us human beings it is *by* virtue that our love is ordered. Virtue is, so to speak, the instrument, ordered love the aim. (*S.T.*, 1*a* 2*ae*, 55.1 *ad* 4). The point that St. Thomas is trying to make by denying that the 'order of love' is, strictly speaking, identical with virtue, and asserting that it is the aim which virtue exists to achieve, is this: 'ordered love', both for Augustine and for Aquinas, is action and inclination about which we can simply say that it is morally good. Augustine was content to speak of virtue as if it were simply morally good action, morally good desires, and so on; but Aquinas here introduces a complication. Virtue, to his mind, is both more and less than goodness in action. Human beings are free agents, and in any given case it is open for a free agent to choose the morally right course from among a large number of alternatives. But some sorts of right action will come more easily, we might almost say more naturally, to some kinds of men. A courageous man, for instance, will be less tempted to run away when he ought to stay at his post than a coward: but both are free to choose to stay, though the decision to do so may cost the coward a more intense struggle: the right choice, for him, goes more 'against the grain' than it does for the brave man. The brave man has a kind of disposition to act bravely: bravery, as we sometimes say, is 'second nature' to him. It is this notion of 'second nature' that Aquinas calls 'virtue'. He describes virtue as a disposition— the word he uses is *habitus*, which is the customary Latin rendering of Aristotle's word *hexis*—but there is really no completely suitable English equivalent; 'habit' will not quite do, though if one thinks of something between 'habit' and 'disposition', it will be near enough, for our purposes, to what he meant by *habitus*. Virtue then, is this sort of thing— I shall go on using the word 'disposition'—a disposition towards morally good action. It follows that there is a whole multitude of virtues: a disposition towards acting courageously—courage; a disposition to avoiding precipitate action, a readiness to wait—patience; and so on. There is a specific virtue for each type of activity, for each distinct capacity in man for activity of a certain kind. Each special virtue disposes the man endowed with that virtue towards correct action of that general type.

This should make it clear why, for Aquinas, virtue is

both more and less than morally good action. It is less, first, because virtue only disposes a man to performing good acts; it is by no means impossible even for a virtuous man to fail, in practice, on some particular occasion, to act in accordance with the good to which his virtue disposes him. In the end, we must judge him by his conduct, not by the disposition which makes it easy or difficult for him to choose one line of conduct rather than another. In this sense, virtue is less than morally good action—and this is why St. Thomas says that it is a means to morally good conduct. But virtue is also more than right conduct. The reason for this is simple. It is possible, at a pinch, to imagine a man who has to struggle against impulses to steal, murder or commit incest on the most trivial occasions. Now even if his struggles were invariably successful, we should regard such a man as one with whom there was something wrong— we should certainly not call him virtuous. Now I have exaggerated in my choice of a ridiculous example; but on a less exaggerated scale, the world is full of people who fairly regularly manage to do the right thing, but with whom this often goes very much against the grain. When we distinguish a virtuous—say a courageous man—from one who just does the right thing, we draw attention to something he *is*, and in a certain sense, this is as important or even more important than what he does. We are saying something about a settled, more or less permanent feature of his character—not about an isolated action of his. He has the kind of character which naturally issues in action appropriate to the virtues he is endowed with. And when we speak about his virtues we draw attention to his settled character, his 'second nature'; and in an important sense we are then doing something more significant than when we are assessing the moral worth of an individual action or group of actions of his.

This notion of virtue is one of the most important things, in my view, that Aquinas learnt from Aristotle. It enabled him to undertake an immensely detailed and subtle analysis of the whole moral life of man, set very firmly within the traditional Christian ideal and indeed within the framework of Augustine's treatment of man on his god-ward journey through the world. Augustine was not interested in the detailed description of the virtues—and of their various kinds of absence, the vices—and indeed, he placed rather more stress on the place of struggle in the moral life. No doubt his sense of the tragic contradictions which belong to the fabric of human living sprang, in part, from his own experience; and this may perhaps be why we often find in the Augustinian emphases something more congenial, something in the end more deeply human. It would, of course, be quite unfair to St. Thomas to suggest that he leaves no place for struggle in his ethics. It is true that the aim of the virtues, on which he lays so much stress, is to make the need for crucial choices less frequent; ideally, right action should come easily, almost naturally, to the virtuous man. But the acquisition of virtue, for Aquinas, too, is a discipline.[1] For virtue, he holds, is established by acting rightly: obviously, *until* the virtue is established by a long succession of right actions of the particular type, action of that type will not *yet* be second nature to the agent, it will go in greater or lesser

[1]This and what follows is true only of human action and virtue in so far as they lie within man's natural capabilities. In so far as a virtue is supernatural, as are the 'theological' virtues of faith, hope, and charity, it is not a product of human discipline but 'caused in us by divine activity' as St. Thomas says (*S.T.*, 1a 2ae, 63.3). Since I have confined myself in this chapter to discussing reason in conduct, it is beyond my scope to discuss these virtues, which 'dispose man towards the good in so far as it is determined by the divine law but lying beyond the reach of human reason' (*ibid.*).

degree against the grain, it will be a struggle. Moral growth is living through this struggle, inevitable as the cost of moral development, that is, of the development of virtue. Morally good conduct, then, is of two kinds, according to the stage of moral development reached by the agent. If he is sufficiently far advanced in virtue for the particular sort of conduct to be done from virtue, from second nature, his action will be expressive of the goodness achieved by him in his own make-up. If he is not far enough advanced, the same action, done 'against the grain', will not be expressive of an already achieved goodness in the agent, but is creative, it contributes to the ultimate achievement of that goodness in him. The ideal is, of course, that all action should flow smoothly from virtue, that it should be expressive of the goodness achieved by the man endowed with all the virtues. But for most of us, this is an ideal; the reality must be very much more a continual questioning of that which comes easily to us, that which is connatural, and a struggle to create in ourselves the good which, we always hope, will one day be fully achieved, and expressed in the actions which flow from it.

We can now understand why St. Thomas insists, with Aristotle, that good action, if it is completely good, is done with pleasure: the reason is that it expresses something in the agent, his character, or second nature—and action which flows from nature is smooth, pleasant: that which is done against nature, does violence to the agent, in some degree—that is to say, is painful. Aquinas does in fact draw the inference that before a man is endowed with the relevant virtue, in performing right actions he has to do himself a certain violence in imposing them on himself. The reason for this—which is another way of saying that the reason why our moral growth and development are necessarily a process of moral struggle—is the fact that there are a multiplicity of faculties, each with its own inclinations, desires, impulses in man, and that these are by no means disciplined by nature. The mind does not enjoy a 'despotic' rule over man's sensual nature, says Aquinas, echoing Aristotle; 'man's desires do not obey the dictates of reason automatically (*omnino ad nutum*), but with some contradiction' (*S.T.*, 1a 2ae, 58.2). If it were true that the mind could straightaway impose the law as it perceives it on man as a whole without any recalcitrance from his baser impulses, then there would be no need for moral virtues. The intellectual virtues, wisdom, knowledge and understanding, would suffice man to gain the knowledge of right and wrong which could, straightaway, be expressed in action. But as things are, man's mind is distracted from true vision of the law under which it stands by the multifarious claims of his sensual nature. The impulses of that nature are rebellious against the law as glimpsed by the mind, and they tend, often, to thwart its feeble attempt to impose order on our disordered nature. The moral virtues are thus required, to help to knit the conflicting impulses and desires into the integrity of a single, whole being. By their means intellectuality, rationality, spirituality—call it what you will—permeates the whole being, and is expressed by the whole person; or, better still, by their means, all that goes to the making of a complete human being, passions, feelings, emotions, desires are all 'intellectualized'; they are taken up into that which is specifically and distinctively human: they are assimilated to rationality.

This concludes what I have wanted to say about the single strand of the Greek inheritance in Christian thought which I chose to look at in the field of ethics: the notion that good and evil in human conduct are somehow bound up with the expression of rationality in action. I have not spoken about the Greek and the Christian moral ideals, the contents of their respective codes—if, in the case of Christianity, especially, one can appropriately speak of a 'code' —in fact I have not dealt at all with the content of morality. I have confined myself to the formal, philosophical accounts of morality as such given by the various thinkers I mentioned. The reasons for this are twofold: first of all, if I had tried to expound the content of the moral law as understood by any one of them, still more by all of them, I would scarcely have scratched the surface yet. Secondly, I do not believe that it is the business of the philosopher to define the content of the moral law. He simply takes what we all know to be good or bad, studies the relations between some of our ideas, and their consequences; and, above all, he asks himself the question we do not normally ask ourselves in practice: granted that such and such things are good, and such and such bad; what do we mean by 'good' and by 'bad'? One aspect of this sort of question we have considered in this chapter. There are other aspects to be looked at, other questions to be asked. To single out the one on which I have focused attention here is to confess, in effect, that, in comparison, their importance is slight. For the cluster of problems associated with this strand of the Christian inheritance from the Greeks has remained central to ethical reflection and inquiry ever since.

9

Time, History, Eternity

THE Greeks were not particularly interested in time, and the things going on in time. According to the prevalent metaphysical tendency of Greek thinking, temporal things are not ultimately real and significant; indeed, it is almost axiomatic for the Greek mind, that such things, the things which come to be and pass away, are not strictly speaking capable of being known at all. We have discussed the view of knowledge which lay behind this position in an earlier chapter. Now we must trace out as far as possible the anti-historical tendencies of such a way of thinking.

The assumption which lies behind this way of thought is that what is ultimately real, as well as what is knowable, is permanent and unchanging. In a world of change and process, there is nothing for the mind to grasp. The substance of the things we see is in perpetual change. Heraclitus, one of the earliest and most obscure of Greek thinkers, expressed this feeling of being haunted by the impermanence of things very clearly: Nothing ever is, everything is becoming; all things are in motion, like streams; so that, to use his image, you cannot step twice into the same river, for fresh waters are always flowing in upon you.[1] Another school of Greek

[1] This traditional interpretation of Heraclitus, followed by

116

thinkers, the followers of Parmenides, worked out the consequences of one side of such a view of the world. Some thinkers of this school would have gone so far as to deny any reality to the things we see around us, subject as they are to change, becoming and decay. They would not have conceded the possibility of any kind of truth in our opinions about them. Some of them drew attention to the contradictions which result from taking this world as real, and our statements about it as true. They concluded that it is illusory, and that we cannot know it or speak about it. We can only know and speak about what is real, 'really real', so to speak. And this really real is incapable of change or movement.

Plato starts with a world which is fundamentally very similar. The goal of the whole of human intellectual activity is to ascend to knowledge of the form of the Good (or the Beautiful, as it appears in some contexts), which is

> first of all, eternal, not subject to becoming and destruction, to growth or decay; which, in the second place, is not beautiful from one point of view, ugly from another, or beautiful at one time and ugly at another, or beautiful to some, ugly to others . . .; but Beauty itself, absolute, simple, and everlasting, in which other beautiful things participate. . . . (*Symp.* 211A–B).

Plato and Aristotle, has recently been questioned as putting the emphasis in the wrong place. G. S. Kirk, in his *Heraclitus: the cosmic fragments* (Cambridge, 1954), suggests that it has diverted attention from the underlying stability of the world which Heraclitus is concerned to assert (pp. 369–80). This may well be true, but does not alter the fact—admitted by Kirk—that Plato did not entirely misunderstand Heraclitus. The flux of things was the primary datum, felt as raising a problem about their permanence and substantial identity.

For Plato the ultimately real world is the unchanging world of the eternal realities which he calls Forms or Ideas. Knowledge, in the strict sense of the term, is possible only of these forms. The pattern on which he conceived genuine knowledge, in the full sense of the word, is that of mathematical knowledge. This is concerned with unchanging, eternal truths, which are not at the mercy of time and change. Mathematics leads the mind from the world of becoming and decay to the contemplation of true being and eternal order.[1]

Plato does not, like Parmenides and some of his followers, condemn the world of becoming and time to unreality and illusion, our statements about it to sheer falsehood and contradiction. He sees in the world of change not something intelligible, or knowable in the strict sense which he gives to this word, but something which participates in, or imitates the real, intelligible world. This imitation, or participation of the real is itself not intelligible, but perceptible: it impinges on us in our ordinary sense-experience; and though we can have no genuine knowledge of it, we can form opinions about it. Opinion is a kind of fleeting half-knowledge of fleeting, half-real things; these are the things of the world around us, always changing, and sensation offers us the only hold we have on them.

Historical knowledge, knowledge of things which go on in time, is necessarily at a discount on such a view. Even Aristotle, whose theory of knowledge does offer us the possibility of genuine knowledge of the material world, cares little for historical inquiry. He does admit the value of history, on account of the lessons which can be learnt from its study. But he qualifies this concession by saying that poetry is 'more scientific' and hence 'superior' to history,

[1] See above, pp. 61–67.

because history is concerned with mere collections of empirical facts, whereas poetry extracts a universal truth from such facts (*Poetica*, 1451b 6–7).

This is a deep-seated attitude common to the majority of Greek philosophers. In the case of many of them, it finds explicit expression in the views they held of time and of history. This is certainly the case with Plato and with Aristotle. Plato formulates his theory of time in the dialogue by which he was to become best known in the early Christian world, the *Timaeus*. In this work, one particularly difficult and controversial to interpret in many of its details, he describes how the divine Craftsman constructed the world on the pattern of the eternal forms 'laid up in heaven'. The Craftsman's task was thus to express as well as may be the eternity of the model in the temporality of the copy; for the character of eternity, which belongs to the pattern, so Plato held, could not be conferred in its fullness on the created copy. Time, therefore, came into being as an image of eternity; the latter indivisible and unnumbered, the former divided and numbered. Time is divided into the three modes of past, present and future, and is measured by number. No time can exist without some regularly recurrent unit of measurement, and such units, again, cannot exist without the regular movement of the heavenly bodies. The regular, perfect, circular motion of this celestial clock is the nearest temporal approximation to and the closest imitation of eternity. The perfect motion of the heavenly bodies being circular, the temporal process which mirrors it is also circular (*Timaeus*, 37C–38C). All living beings go through the familiar cycle of birth, growth, maturity, decay and death; and the same applies to the whole of the created universe, both in its parts and as a whole. Everything revolves in time according to number, and time itself revolves as the

C.F.–I

first of the moving things. The cycles are repeated until the whole cosmic cycle is fulfilled in the Great Year, that is to say, until the time when all the heavenly bodies, and hence the rest of the constituents of the cosmos, find themselves in the same relation to one another as they were at the beginning. And then a new cycle begins. There is no end to this recurrent cycle of cosmic change, endlessly repeating itself, events succeeding one another in the same order indefinitely.

Aristotle's view of time is very similar. In his account of the universe, too, the heavenly spheres in their perfect regular, circular movement imitate the eternity of the timeless being at the summit of the system. This is the 'unmoved mover' (or movers) described as 'thought thinking itself' (*Met.* Λ, 1074b34), symbolized by a circle. As a result, for Aristotle, too, all change is cyclic. For if the movement of the heavens is periodic, so must be the effects produced by it. This is as true of human as of cosmic activity; even the opinions of philosophers will recur in the same forms and in the same order, 'not once or twice nor a few times, but indefinitely' (*Meteora*, 339b29). Aristotle, it is true, mitigates the determinism of this view by making it clear that the periodically recurrent events are specifically, not individually identical. This explains why many Greek thinkers, Plato not least, could combine such a cyclic, deterministic cosmology with a deep sense of individual human destiny. The expression of this awareness by Stoic and Neoplatonic thinkers like Epictetus, Seneca, Proclus and others sometimes approaches the Christian sense of 'waiting upon God'. Nor was the cyclic picture of temporal process incompatible with holding 'progressive' views about particular phases of the cycle.[1] The idea of the cycles of existence, whatever the

[1] cp. W. K. C. Guthrie, *In the beginning* (London, 1957), Chs. 4 and 5.

colouring of their attitude to it, pessimistic or optimistic, commended itself very strongly to Greek thinkers. Even when particular philosophers allowed the possibility of an escape from the cycle, this was conceived in individual, personal terms. There could be no conception of a people chosen for salvation or deliverance, for the large-scale pattern of history could not allow this. Salvation could only be conceived as being *from* history.

Aristotle may have done no more than to press such a theory of time to its logical conclusion when he pointed out that if it is taken seriously, even the notions of 'before' and 'after' become purely relative. For if all events are located on a circle, there is no reason why we should say, for instance, that we live after the men of Troy rather than before them: if one goes far enough round the circle, what appears anterior approached from one direction, is posterior when approached from the other (*Probl.* 916a18ff.). Aristotle and Plato were both giving philosophical expression to a very widely held view of time. In Christian times its most popular representative was probably the Stoic theory, according to which at the end of each cosmic cycle the world would be reabsorbed into the fire which pervades all matter in a great world-conflagration. The picture of time behind the theory is the same. It may be that this picture of the world-process has its roots among the deepest springs of human thinking.[1] For the Greek mind, at any rate, it expressed the nature of its scientific ideal: to know the cosmic process as a whole, to render nature wholly transparent to understanding. All particulars were to be understood in terms of universal law; and if universal law was to be supreme, there was no room for the unique,

[1]cp. M. Eliade, *The myth of the eternal return* (E. Tr.) (London, 1955).

concrete historical event considered in its uniqueness, as a fit subject for rational inquiry.

Against the background of a vision of time such as this, it is difficult to see how history can become in any sense significant. There is nothing decisive, nothing finally achieved, only endless repetition. Necessity governs the whole cosmic process, and often even the individual human soul and human activity are made subject to the perpetual return to the same point which runs through the world-process. There is no state of definitive rest, of accomplished task and fulfilled destiny; the only escape from the 'sorrowful wheel of life' is escape from the world of time into contemplation of the timeless truths.

And yet, it was against such a background that scientific history was first written. Herodotus has sometimes been dismissed as a gossip-writer and gatherer of outlandish lore from all parts of the world known to him. Even in antiquity, his reputation as the 'father of history' was often eclipsed: Cicero was not alone in calling him a liar, a story-teller. But the choice of the word *historia* in Herodotus' own description of his work points to something very different. Before his time, the word, meaning 'investigation', had been used with reference to philosophical inquiry. With Herodotus legend-writing had become superseded by historical investigation. His lively interest in history, and a deep concern for accuracy within the limits of his information, cannot be mistaken. But if it would be pointless to complain that he does not use modern methods of historical scholarship, it may be worth suggesting that he did share the presuppositions of contemporary 'scientific' activity. In his very claim to put history on a scientific basis, is implied an acceptance of what constitutes the hall-mark of scientific work: and this, for the Greeks, consisted above all, in the discovery of the law or pattern behind events.

Herodotus was too much of a historian to allow himself to be carried away by the fascination of patterns from interest in events. But he shares the scientific ideal of his time to a sufficient extent to construct his narrative in such a way as to display the pattern into which they fit. It has been suggested[1] that Herodotus saw historical process in terms of the same categories as those which Heraclitus had applied to the cosmic process. Heraclitus saw behind the flux of events a *logos*, a rational principle, the apprehension of which, he thought, was the apprehension of the eternal wisdom which governs all things. This *logos* is conceived of as a universal principle of natural justice. According to it all things and events have their assigned place in the course of nature, excesses and deficiencies being compensated by nature. The element of stability in the world is the result of a 'harmony of opposites', in virtue of which tension, strife and opposition are held in equilibrium.

The workings of this cosmic principle of natural justice have been discerned in historical events as narrated by Herodotus. It is true that he appears to follow something like this Heraclitean principle of compensation in some of his explanations of natural phenomena, as, for instance, of the flooding of the Nile. But Herodotus is too lively to be confined in such a philosophic straitjacket. He does share the prevalent Greek liking for a pattern, even a law of some general kind, behind events. It is no more necessary, however, to identify this with the *logos* of Ionian cosmology than it is to see this *logos* at work in the pattern of *hubris* and

[1]This view of Herodotus is taken by C. N. Cochrane in his excellent book, *Christianity and classical culture* (Oxford, 1940), pp. 458ff.

nemesis in Greek tragedy. If we cannot assert, on the one hand, that history, for Herodotus, is a kind of large-scale, human version of Ionian cosmology, nor can we assert, on the other, that his history is a simple narrative, 'wie es eigentlich geschehen ist'. The pattern into which it is carefully fitted is all important. Thus Herodotus is fond of presenting adversity as the penalty for wrong-doing; and the over-all pattern of his theme, the struggle between Greece and Persia, is envisaged as the culminating phase of a perpetual conflict between West and East. The forces of conflict are the eastward and westward movements always present in history; the earlier books display them at work in a series of raids and retaliatory raids to compensate for them. There is nothing unique or even abnormal about the final *dénouement* in the expedition of Xerxes: it is part of the perpetual dialectic of historical process as Herodotus sees it. There is an air of inevitability about it, by the time one has read the preceding books of Herodotus' history. It was easy for a fifth-century Greek historian to see the catastrophic changes of fortune of his time in a pattern of conflicting opposites and compensation for excess. It was only a short step from the consciousness of a pattern of change from one state to its opposite—from smallness to greatness, from happiness to misery, from pride to abasement—to a vision of historical study as an attempt to discover the law of the process. Aristotle went very little beyond Herodotus when he explicitly justified history on the grounds of the lessons it taught. In the pattern of his historical writing the rhythm of life always repeats itself, and the past is worth recalling to give one a clue to the future course of events.

Thucydides' claim to the name of a historian has been even more sharply contested than that of Herodotus,[1] but

[1] e.g. by R. G. Collingwood, who writes: 'He (Thucydides) has

perhaps with even less justification. It is true that in the speeches, for instance, which he puts in the mouths of his characters, there is no attempt to achieve historical verisimilitude. They are what the historian considers to have been likely, the words a man would have spoken if placed in the given circumstances. Thucydides' reliance on contemporary testimony, however, should be enough to defend him against the charge of being more interested in psychological laws than in history. In his work the historian, the moralist, the psychologist, and at times even the prophet, all join hands; and they are never far from the philosopher's concern to understand, and to understand in terms of the timeless categories of law and pattern.

In the work of Herodotus and of Thucydides we can see the beginnings of a genuine intellectual discipline, that of history. It is scarcely surprising that this discipline should have arrived on the scene entangled with interests of another kind, the presuppositions and methods of other intellectual disciplines. In view of the anti-historical outlook of Greek philosophic consciousness, what is surprising is that it did not mould itself to the pattern of something other than history—something more like the Greek notion of serious intellectual activity—more than it did.

In contrast with the intellectual climate of classical Greece and its later, Hellenistic expressions, the Christian and Jewish mind is interested in events rather than in the

---

a bad conscience. He is trying to justify himself for writing history at all by turning it into something that is not history . . . Herodotus may be the father of history, but Thucydides is the father of psychological history. Now what is psychological history? It is not history at all, but natural science of a special kind. It does not narrate facts for the sake of narrating facts. Its chief purpose is to affirm laws, psychological laws' (*The idea of history*, Oxford, 1946, p. 29).

laws and patterns into which they fit. All events, the most trivial no less than the world-shaking, fall under God's providential care. Their ultimate significance is the place they occupy in his providential order. It is their very uniqueness and concreteness—their unintelligible residue, for the prevailing Greek temper of thought—which is significant. The Bible's concern is not with ideas or eternal truths or general laws, but with people, their lives, what they did, what happened. The Bible was seen, both by Judaism and by Christianity, first and foremost as a historical record. It contained the history of God's dealings with men, concentrated in the history of his chosen people, the Jews. On the face of it, at any rate, the Bible *is* history. It is full of temporal categories of thought: creation, destiny—of the tribe as well as of the individual—promise, prophecy, waiting, hope, fulfilment and realization. A faith based on the Bible necessarily implies a relation to the past and future as well as to the present.

Pagan controversialists such as Celsus and Porphyry were quick to appreciate how deeply the Christian faith cut across the established categories of thought. Its professed involvement in historical events as the foundation of its faith, its valuation of history as the medium of salvation and its belief in the final vindication of history, were utterly unacceptable to them. This appears clearly in the doctrines they single out most consistently for rejection: the idea of God made man, suffering and dying for men, and the promise that men would rise again bodily. And St. Augustine, looking back upon what he thought best in pagan thought, could find much of Christian teaching anticipated by it; but even his ingenuity failed to detect an anticipation in pagan thought of the distinctive events of the Christian redemption-history.

The conceptual equipment inherited by Christian thinkers from antiquity was of little use in helping them to formulate their understanding of time and history. They did, however, find in this heritage from classical thought all they required to formulate their sense of the eternity of the Lord of history. In the Bible, God is everywhere at work in human history. He deals with nations according to his will, he is angry or merciful, and even changes his mind. The Greeks, in identifying the most fully real with the unchanging, the most fully alive with the timeless perfection of supreme being, had paved the way for Christian thinkers when they came to face the task of expressing in more sophisticated terms what even the Biblical imagery suggested, what its variety converged towards and pointed to:

> Ground of being, and granite of it: past all
>   Grasp God, throned behind
> Death with a sovereignty that heeds but hides, bodes but
>   abides.

The Greek contribution to Christian theological talk about God's eternity has been so inwardly assimilated that most theologians are scarcely aware of it. The language of philosophy has entered that of religion so completely that not until our own day has its strangeness to the Bible's language been noticed.

Eternity is not, then, a Biblical concept,[1] though it is one

[1] It is not, at any rate, present in the Bible as a developed concept. The Fourth Gospel's conception of 'eternal life' contains elements of the notion of 'eternity', and Professor C. H. Dodd has suggested that 'it is evident that when Philo uses the term $\zeta \omega \dot{\eta}$ $\alpha i \dot{\omega} \nu \iota o s$ (*de Fuga*, 78), he means by it a life which, like that of God, is "eternal" in the sense of timeless. The thought of the Fourth Gospel has . . . some affinity with that of Philo. It appears that

which may help the Christian thinker in his attempt to
understand the Biblical *datum*; time and history, in contrast, are notions at the very heart of the Biblical revelation.[1]
Not only do time and history come into their own in the
Biblical perspective; but they assume a peculiar significance,
a significance based on the divine activity of which they are
the medium.

In the Old Testament, time is a straight line. There is
a true beginning—Creation—and an end, the final winding
up of temporal history. It is true, that at both ends this
straight line ended in a kind of indeterminate region,
shrouded in mist: the Hebrew mind was so closely bound to
the dimension of history that it could not readily conceive
of a 'before' or an 'after' history. Let us diagrammatically
represent this Hebrew picture as in Fig. 1:

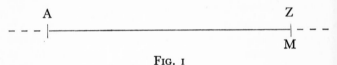

FIG. 1

he too means by ζωή αἰώνιος "eternal life" in the Platonic sense,
at least so far, that it is a life not measured by months and years,
a life which has neither past nor future, but is lived in God's
eternal To-day'. (*The Fourth Gospel*, Cambridge, 1955, p. 150).
Professor Dodd's qualification, however, is noteworthy: 'In thus
bringing the concept of ζωή αἰώνιος into the context of Greek
philosophical thought, the evangelist has, however, avoided the
abstract and static quality which adheres to Greek and Hellenistic
"mysticism". . . . Here the affiliation of his thought to Hebraic
antecedents is of importance, for the Hebrew conception of life is
always one of action, movement and enjoyment.' (*ibid.*)

[1] On the Christian understanding of time, see O. Cullmann,
Christ and time (E. Tr.) (London, 1951). What I have to say on this
topic leans heavily—as most things written since its appearance—
on Cullmann's great work. See also J. Daniélou, *The Lord of
history* (E. Tr.) (London, 1958).

Time begins with a Genesis, a birth, a coming to be (A), and it ends with the final winding up of history, when all human destiny is fulfilled in a reign of peace and justice (Z). Gradually the conception of a Messiah, a saviour who was somehow to establish this reign of peace and justice, became more definite, and the inauguration of his kingdom was seen as coinciding with this end (M). The whole process is a story of men in God's sight, subject to his providence. The conception of God's providence, his *pronoia*—his 'foreseeing thought', to render it as literally as possible—points the sharp contrast between the Biblical and the Greek assessments of history. Providence is not a universal law immanent in the world process, but a concern with each unique event and action. It is a sovereign freedom which concerns itself with other free acts and agents. It is in its sight that events and actions receive their real significance. Time—*chronos*—becomes, in the Bible, a series of *kairoi*—of opportune moments in God's sight. Oscar Cullmann, in his great work, *Christ and time*, has drawn attention to the way in which the New Testament is full of time words: 'the hour', 'the day', 'the fullness of time', 'the acceptable time'; even its oppositions between our world and the world to come is drawn in temporal terms: 'the present age' and 'the age to come'. Where we should be tempted to speak of a 'here below' and a 'beyond', the Bible prefers to speak of a 'before' and 'after'. And God is not only intimately concerned with all that happens in the course of this history: he himself, according to the Christian belief, bursts into it.

God's irruption into history in the Incarnation of his Son is the distinctively Christian belief. My purpose here is not to defend it, but to see what happens to the Biblical picture of time if it is accepted. The time scheme, represented in Fig. 1 is something that Christianity shares, fundamentally, with Judaism. For both, time begins with the creation, and ends with the *eschaton*, the 'end'. The *eschaton* is the final winding up of terrestrial history, in the fullness of time. But —and this is the staggering new claim—the Christian believes that the Messiah promised to the Jews in the fullness of time has already come; that the promises made to the chosen people, and the prophecies of the Old Testament have already been fulfilled. To display this, our diagram of the Old Testament time scheme has thus to be revised according to the way it was seen by Christians:

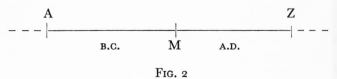

FIG. 2

In the Old Testament perspective, history began with the creation and ended with the advent of the Messiah and the establishment of his kingdom. In the Incarnation, death and resurrection of its Lord, the primitive Christian community saw this end as having already arrived. This is why they lived in anguished expectation of an imminent end to temporal history; it is also why—from this point of view— it was so difficult for a Jew to accept the Christian claims: he would appreciate their cataclysmic significance: if they were true, the end had come; whereas, as was becoming increasingly clearer, history was still going on. Slowly the realization grew in the early Church that life 'in the last times'—that is to say until the return of the Lord in glory and the in-gathering of his faithful from the ends of the earth to share his glory—might go on indefinitely. The delay in the *parousia*, the glorious return of the Lord, failed, in the last resort, to shake their faith in Jesus as Messiah. Instead it accustomed them to a new scheme of time in history. Cullmann has shown the implications of this radical novelty. The end had already come, at the mid-point of history: the promise and the prophecies were fulfilled, God's saving work among men had been accomplished. And yet, paradoxically, it was also still to come: the already accomplished fulfilment had to be finally clinched, men still had to avail themselves of the redemption already wrought by God in Christ. The Incarnation has introduced a dislocation into the original time-scheme of the Bible: with bringing the end into the middle, there is a wrench in the line. This wrench in the time-scheme of history is reflected, for Christians, in their attitude to the time they live in. It is a time of tension; of tension between a past which is always present, and a future which is already, radically, present.

Time, in Christian thought, is conceived as moving in a straight line, or, more precisely, in a broken straight line, or two lines, as expressed in our reckoning of time B.C. and A.D. The break with the classical Greek cyclic view of history could not be more complete; and early Christian theologians are unanimous in their protests against it. In the cyclic view of history and the assertion of recurrence, men like Origen and Augustine saw a denial of significance to human responsibility, an assertion of final triviality. What for the Greeks had been the unknowable residue of scientific knowledge, was seen by Christianity as the vehicle of divine meaning and saving action. This divergence in their respective valuations of historical existence displays very conspicuously the break between Christianity and Classicism.

The historian's concern is with the ever changing world of men, their activity, its conditions, its results. We have now seen something of the Bible's way of understanding the strand of history which it recounts, and the time-scheme in which it displays the significance of the events of which the sacred history consists. But what of the rest of human history, the history of peoples who do not come within the purview of the Biblical history, the history of the twenty or so centuries since the completion of the Bible? Christian thinkers have, of course, gone on reflecting on history ever since. Sometimes, just like other men, they have thought to discern recurrent patterns in the course of events, or laws that events allegedly obey. In so doing, they have usually drawn the fire not only of other historians, with rival patterns to canvass, or of philosophical critics of historical pattern-tracing like Sir Isaiah Berlin and Professor K. R. Popper; but the Christian theologian, too, is often, and rightly, very much on edge in the presence of any proposed pattern or law of recurrent events. For him history must in the end, remain full of the mystery of God's unfathomable purposes. For our limited, human awareness, these are embodied in the brute giveness of what actually happens. This is why there can be no Christian philosophy of history in the 'pattern-making' sense. There is no Christian pattern; indeed, in an important sense, Christianity is the very negation of pattern. There is only the infinitely complex interplay of the factors which shape the course of events— and to unravel these is the task of historical scholarship. All that the Christian theologian can do is to set history within the providential plan of the economy of the redemption: but in doing so, he is leaving the field of philosophy, and is offering what can only be called a theology of history. St. Augustine, engaged in writing his great work the *City of God* during the very years which saw the crumbling of the Roman Empire, was keenly aware of this. That whole vast enterprise of his may be looked at, from one point of view, as the rejection of the classical view of history and his attempt to fill the gap created by that rejection. In the stark opposition of sin and holiness he sees the simple categories of the ultimate judgement on human enterprise, individual and social alike; and yet, his whole weight is thrown into the insistence that the application of these simple categories to the complex fabric of empirical history is always a matter of perplexity and doubt. The two cities are inextricably intertwined in this world, and their destinies will not be known to us until their manifestation in the last judgement.[1] The image of the career of two cities inseparably woven into the one fabric of empirical history serves a twofold purpose in Augustine: it provides him both with a scheme for the interpretation of human history and, at the same time, for the assertion of its irreducible complexity defying all merely human attempts at interpretation. Christian theologians and historians have sometimes been ready to apply Augustine's categories to history without his concern to safeguard their transcendence; without sharing the agnostic humility of his refusal to see deeper into the mystery of God's working in history than God himself has revealed. Their more simple-minded approach has often led them to display the skein of history as already, before our eyes, wound off 'all on two spools'. Even Augustine's immediate disciple, Orosius, cannot be wholly absolved from such a charge. But in Augustine's deepest insight history is set free from its bondage to philosophy. The

[1]cp. C. Dawson, 'St. Augustine and the City of God', in *The Dynamics of world history* (London, 1957), pp. 294–325. (Reprinted from *A monument to St. Augustine*, London, 1930.) On this topic, see also the distinguished paper read at the Second International Conference on Patristic Studies (Oxford, 1955), by H.-I. Marrou. ('Civitas Dei, civitas terrena: num tertium quid?' In *Studia patristica*, edited by K. Aland and F. L. Cross (Berlin, 1957), Vol. 2, pp. 342–50.)

historian's autonomy is vindicated against the claims of the philosophical weavers of patterns; and yet, the setting and ultimate significance of all human action is ever-present. Christianity has made it possible to reject a philosophy of history and to substitute for it a theology.

10

Faith and Philosophy

WE have discussed a number of topics, with an eye to discovering what Christian thinkers took from Greek philosophy, and what they made of it in their own work. At several points we noticed elements of Greek reflection which could not find a place in Christian thought; in general, however, we have concentrated on those aspects of Greek philosophy which did become important within a Christian framework, and we have noticed that there was indeed a very great deal of it. Some of it had to undergo more or less drastic revision in the course of being pressed into service for Christian purposes, much of it had simply to be placed in a new context, the context of the Christian religion. Now we must turn to some of the central problems connected with the fact that so much Greek speculation should have proved capable of being assimilated by Christian thinkers.

First, it is important to appreciate that there is a problem here. Throughout the age of the Fathers of the Church, the medieval scholastics, the Reformation—in fact in all the ages of great theological activity or renewal—it has always been taken for granted by Christian thinkers that the content of the Christian faith is a God-given revelation. In the Word of God incarnate, God had communicated his saving

truth to men; the Bible contained the record of his revelation—both its preparatory stages in the history of his chosen
people, and its consummation in the life, work and teaching
of Jesus Christ. In this revelation was made known to men
the way, the truth and the life: and men had no access
other than this to the saving truth which was theirs in faith.
What need was there that men endowed with this saving
faith should turn to pagan thought? And if they did turn
to it, what did it have to offer them? The faith which was
in them was, as they well knew, radically new, beyond the
possibility of the human mind to arrive at of its own power,
by its own activity; it was simply *given*. Speculation, no
matter how deeply concerned with the quest for truth, how
logically acute or poetically inspired, could add nothing to
what God had revealed. Speculation, as a gateway to the
ultimate truth, the truth which forms the object of men's
ultimate concern, had no more to offer. The abrogation of
philosophy as a gateway to saving truth had been stated in
the strongest terms by St. Paul in the contrast he drew
between the wisdom of this world, which is foolishness with
God, and the foolishness of God which is wiser than men,
through which it has pleased God to save those who believe
(I Cor. 1.18–25).

St. Paul's way of opposing the wisdom of men and the
faith in the divine revelation is as uncompromising as one
could wish for; and yet, when visiting Athens, speaking to
Greeks on their home ground, he, too, could point to the
altar of the unknown god and present Christian belief to his
pagan audience as that for which they had been groping
in the dark, the answer to their searchings, and the object
of their mute worship.[1] How did Christian thinkers put

[1] cp. Acts 17.16–34. The authenticity of this passage has been
questioned on the grounds of its allegedly un-Pauline character—

together this twofold insistence of St. Paul's: the insistence, on the one hand, on the radical novelty and utter trans- cendence of faith in Christ, its unattainability by human initiative, and the insistence, on the other hand, that some- how, human speculation could find a home within faith?

The process of reconciling these two positions within Christian thinking was gradual; and at the beginning, at any rate, hesitant, perplexed and not without setbacks. Even once a solution had been worked out, every major intellectual upheaval in Christendom has tended to pre- cipitate a new crisis, when the solutions achieved were inevitably questioned, and had to be re-established in an altered context. For the present, we shall confine our atten- tion to the first of such crises, that precipitated by the original encounter of Christianity with the Greek intellec- tual world. Taking this first encounter in a fairly broad sense, we shall be looking at it as stretching from roughly the end of the first century to the early fifth century. The reason for choosing the end of the first century as the point of departure is that by this date Christian missionaries were travelling around the Mediterranean countries, proclaiming a message fairly definite in its content, becoming known in the predominantly Greek-speaking world, and establishing communities in many of its urban centres. The mere fact that the new faith had to make its message heard in Greek as well as in the native language of its country of origin meant that it was brought face to face with Greek civiliza- tion; and this inevitably meant, sooner or later, with Greek philosophy as well. The early fifth century is a suitable

---

cp. M. Dibelius, *Studies in the Acts of the Apostles* (E. Tr.), London, 1956, pp. 63ff. In the absence of other grounds, this *a priori* rejec- tion of such complexity in the Pauline position seems quite un- warranted.

point at which to locate the end of this first crisis of confrontation. For from whatever point of view one considers the intellectual history of early Christianity, the figure of St. Augustine towers over it, marking the end of a civilization and, in very large measure, helping to create the new one which was to emerge from the ruins.

Quite early in the history of the Church there were Christian thinkers who stressed exclusively the novelty of Christianity, the fact that faith in Christ is utterly beyond the reach of human knowledge. In a sense they are extremists; it is easy to parody their insistence on the transcendence of faith by suggesting that

> 'since God has spoken to us, it is no longer necessary for us to think. The only thing that matters for every one of us', so this parody might run, 'is to achieve his own salvation: now all that we need to know in order to achieve it is there, written down in the Holy Scriptures; let us therefore read the divine law, meditate upon it, live according to its precepts, and we shall stand in need of nothing else, not even of philosophy. I should rather say: particularly *not* of philosophy. In point of fact we shall do infinitely better without philosophical knowledge than with it.'[1]

A good many early Christian thinkers did talk in just such terms. A remarkable instance is that of Tatian, an eastern convert to Christianity in the middle of the second century, who had had a philosophic training of a kind. He glories in the 'barbarity' of Christianity—this is what fixes a gulf between its saving truth and the errors of all the philosophers. 'For what great and wonderful things have all

[1] Quoted from E. Gilson, *Reason and revelation in the Middle Ages* (New York, 1952), p. 6.

your philosophers brought about?' he asks the Greeks (*Or.* 25): they all disagree among each other, delight in confusing the mind with labyrinthine argumentation, adopt ridiculous forms of life and know not the truth. And for Tatian, this attitude to Greek philosophy was part and parcel of his total assessment of Greek civilization, upon which his work is a sustained onslaught. Much of Tatian's language is echoed by the words of a very much greater thinker writing some half a century later, Tertullian.

For all Tertullian's brilliance of intellect, for all his importance in helping to form the theological language of Latin Christendom, and—we might add—for all his unacknowledged indebtedness to various strands of Greek philosophic thought—what we find in his writings is the same uncompromising opposition to pagan philosophy. 'What is there in common between the philosopher and the Christian?' he asks. 'What between the disciple of Greece and the disciple of heaven? . . ., the friend and the enemy of error?' (*Apol.* 46). The philosophers, he says, 'are rash interpreters of the divine nature and dispensation', they are the fountainhead of all the heresies; that is why St. Paul warns the Colossians lest they be seduced by their empty speculations. For 'what has Athens to do with Jerusalem? The Academy with the Church? Heresy with Christianity? . . . we must seek the Lord in purity of heart . . . since Christ Jesus there is no room for further curiosity, since the Gospel no need for further research. If we believe, let us not desire to find further belief' (*Praescr.* 7). He remembers, of course, that Christ says in the Gospel 'seek and ye shall find', 'knock and it shall be opened unto you' (Matt. 7.7–8 = Luke 11.9–10); but his remarks on these sayings are significant: they were addressed, he says, by Jesus to the Jews, at the beginning of his ministry, before they had been shown sufficient evidence to prove him to be the expected Messiah. There is no need for us, who accept him as the Saviour, to seek any more. And even if we were to take the saying as addressed to all men, it would have to be interpreted, Tertullian insists, as meaning 'seek until you find, believe when you have found, and then hold on to what you have found, believing in addition only that nothing else is to be believed, nor sought after when you have found and believed that which has been instituted by him who has commanded you to seek only what he has instituted' (*Praescr.* 8–9). In professing his belief in the things which constitute the chief stumbling blocks to his pagan readers, Tertullian underlines the breach between the two intellectual worlds: 'The Son of God is crucified: I am not ashamed, because it is shameful; the Son of God died: it is credible, because it is absurd; the Son of God was buried and rose again: it is certain because it is impossible' (*De carne Christi*, 5).

Tertullian has been quoted at some length because in him appears the finest classical expression of this point of view. It is easy to parody the intransigence of this kind of view, and to disown it without pausing to note its deeper significance. For in the second century, as at many other times, it was easy to fail to appreciate the radical novelty of Christianity, the absolute gulf between the truth which it claimed had been revealed by God in Christ, and the utmost possibilities of human reflection. One of the religious movements which had in the second century become so widespread that it constituted a very real threat to Christian orthodoxy, the movement, or rather group of movements, which we nowadays group together under the title 'gnosticism', was based on just such a failure. The origins of these sects and their doctrines are still not fully known, though a

good deal of material has recently come to light on them.[1]
They certainly contained a very great deal taken from
Greek, Jewish and other near-Eastern sources, philosophy,
mythology, and the basic religious impulse behind it all.
Yet, their claim was that their teaching expressed the
authentic nature of Christianity. The Biblical faith of the
ordinary, uninstructed members of the community, they
held was all very well for the multitude; but the *élite*, the
'spiritual' Christians, as some of them were fond of calling
themselves, knew better. They had a further insight, beyond the simple faith: *gnosis*, knowledge. And although in
some cases the fundamentally Christian inspiration of their
thought is inescapable, the unique character of their faith
is invariably compromised. The persons and events of the
Gospel become incorporated in a kind of cosmic dramatic
myth, and lose their real, historical character. Out of
Christian belief, along with other ingredients, the gnostics
constructed their various accounts of saving truth. They
often did owe some features, some of the conceptual scaffold-
ing of their systems, to late Stoic and Platonic philosophy.
Christian controversialists certainly suggested that all their
heresies were drawn from following the philosophers rather
than the Scriptures and the tradition of the Church. They
seem to have exaggerated the gnostics' philosophical indebtedness to paganism—but they were fundamentally
right in seeing so clearly that thinking of this type compromised the uniqueness, the givenness of the Gospel. If one

---

[1]For a general discussion of the new material, see F. L. Cross,
Ed., *The Jung Codex* (London, 1955); G. Quispel, *Gnosis als Welt-
religion* (Zürich, 1951); and my article, 'New evidence on Gnosticism', in *Blackfriars* 36 (1955), pp. 209–16. References to other
accounts are also given in Quispel's book, and in my article referred
to in note 1, p. 147. On gnostic origins the most complete recent
discussion is R. McL. Wilson, *The gnostic problem* (London, 1958).

reads Tertullian's protest against this kind of background, one must give him credit for a powerful re-statement of this uniqueness and givenness of the saving faith, even though one must then go on to disown his violent rejection of all pagan thinking.

The views voiced by Tatian and Tertullian were not, of course, the only Christian views, even in the second century. There were two needs which made themselves felt, both of which made it necessary for Christian thinkers to face the task of reaching some *modus vivendi* with pagan philosophy.

First, there was the need to make the new faith comprehensible to the contemporary mind; and in so far as the contemporary intellectual world was permeated with Stoic and Platonic ideas, this meant reaching some sort of understanding with Stoicism and Platonism. It was a delicate task, because it was a matter of formulating their sense of the meaning of the teaching, life, death and resurrection of Jesus in terms which would record with strict fidelity the sense of Scripture. Secondly, there was the simple fact that quite soon educated men began to be found within the community of Christian converts. It was inevitable that some of these men should ask themselves how the intellectual equipment which they had brought with them from their pagan education could find a place, and even a useful function within the Church. There seem to have been a number of lines along which they tried to answer these questions. They are in fact often not very clearly separated, and often more than one approach is found in the work of one thinker.

One common way of bridging the gap between philosophy and faith lay in suggesting that all that was true and valuable in the work of the philosophers had been borrowed by them from the Hebrew Scriptures, back in the misty past. Plato had been a disciple of Moses, or of the prophets, and had borrowed from their writings the glimpses he had of the truth. Philosophers had no independent access to truth. All that was their own were the interpolated errors, the distortions of the truth, the misunderstanding of the divine revelation. These were so manifold that they produced the multiplicity of philosophical schools, which, in their turn, gave rise to the multiplicity of heretical sects in the Church. Obviously, this is a make-shift solution, and would not bear serious scrutiny. Although it lingered on for quite a time—there are traces of it even in St. Augustine— it soon ceased to have any importance as the means of Christian acceptance of pagan thought.

There was a second, and much more profound line along which some Christian thinkers tried to work out a solution. The crude view just mentioned held that the element of truth in pagan thought was the residue of a revelation: philosophy could claim to be true just in so far, as it was in the last resort, in fact faith. Human reason could bring nothing but error and distortion to dilute the truth of faith. The view first put forward by St. Justin Martyr round about the middle of the second century, was a radical departure from this. Instead of saying that all truth came from revelation, he admitted that human reason had access to truth, even though, being human, it often fell into error. Here Justin has recourse to the Stoic teaching about the *logos spermatikos*, the 'seminal word'. In the Stoic picture, the universe was wholly permeated by a cosmic reason, a *logos*. Justin maintained that all those before Christ who lived 'with the logos', were basically Christians (I *Apol.* 46). This *logos* disseminated among all men at all times is a kind of fragmentary anticipation and participation of the whole truth which was revealed in the *Logos* made flesh, in the Word of God incarnate. The fullness of the truth is disclosed only in Christ; but those who lived and thought in accordance with the disseminated *logos*, even if knowing nothing of Christ, lived and thought in accordance with the truth (II *Apol.* 8, 13). This is the first serious attempt in the history of Christian thinking to come to terms with pagan philosophy by representing the best of pagan thought as part of the 'preparation of the Gospel'.

This theory does, indeed, bridge the gulf between Christian faith and pagan thought. But one may well ask whether it does not, in building a bridge, almost do away with the gulf to be bridged. Tertullian, as we noticed, stressed quite uncompromisingly the absolute novelty of faith in a God-given revelation, its complete strangeness to all merely human revelation. Will it really do, if, following Justin, we say that this novelty, this strangeness of Christianity is just that it is the whole, whereas all that came before had been partial? Can we really be content with seeing the relation between faith and philosophy as one of whole to part?

I think not; and I shall have opportunity later on to suggest that the importance of this position lies elsewhere. For the present, we must examine the third fundamental type of view which Christian thinkers took of the relation of faith and reason. This was first sketched by Saint Irenaeus, who wrote a generation or so after Justin. Irenaeus was not interested in philosophy, as Justin had been. He was very much a working bishop, deeply concerned to protect his flock against the seductive persuasiveness of gnosticism in all its varied forms. His answer was so clear and so simple and it has become so completely accepted in the whole Christian theological tradition, that we may well fail to appreciate how revolutionary it was. It consisted quite simply of two firm positions: first, that human thinking, valuable and truthful though it may be, is impotent to know God and his dispensation for the salvation of men. He saw gnosticism fundamentally as a human attempt to arrive at this saving knowledge by its own efforts. Secondly he insisted that salvation was only to be attained through faith in what God had revealed, and more important still, in what he had done. Human reason and divine revelation were, so to speak, in different dimensions, much in the way in which we saw *eros* to be man's love directed to God, and *agape* God's towards man. Man's intellectual quest, no matter how far-reaching, can never become God's own self-communication in revelation, nor can it be a substitute for it. The gnostics, even though they may often, outwardly at least, have accepted much of Christian teaching, treated it always as on a par with all the other ingredients, philosophical and mythological, which they incorporated in their system. Against their challenge Irenaeus came to see and to state the true relation of human thought and faith in a Christian mind. This had simply to be one of complete, unreserved and unconditional acceptance of revelation. Once that is assured, all freedom is vouchsafed to Christian thought—it can draw on any philosophical or other kind of insight to deepen its understanding of what it believes by faith. God had revealed himself in his saving action in human history: the Biblical record of this revelation defined the content of the Christian's faith. All his thinking and life had to be founded on this faith: the revelation is the unconditionally accepted framework within which he carries on his human thinking, its *point de départ*. The task of the theologian, as Irenaeus states it, is just that of bringing to bear on the content of the Christian faith whatever intellectual equipment he may be endowed with. This may range from something as rudimentary as attempting to understand the words of the Scriptures to very much more sophisticated kinds of intellectual activity, in which the pattern and coherence of revelation is scrutinized, or the whole range of a man's vision of the world is brought into relation with faith. In being thus brought into play as part of the intellectual equipment with which a man tries to grasp revelation, or penetrate deeper into his faith, philosophy becomes theology. Although Irenaeus was not himself very interested in philosophy, this is implied by his position. He would have seen no reason to repudiate the addition of philosophy to the intellectual disciplines he regarded as capable of having theological relevance.

It used to be said—especially by theologians of the school of Adolf von Harnack—that the only difference between gnostic heresy and Christian orthodoxy lay in the fact that gnosticism undertook a radical hellenization of Christianity, whereas orthodoxy underwent and accepted a gradual, slow process of hellenization. What such a statement leaves out is the factor which seemed vital to a man like Irenaeus: it was not a matter of speed or extent to which Greek thought-forms were admissible within Christianity; no one is more liberal in the scope he allows to human thinking in the context of faith than Irenaeus. His point is that in theology all this thinking is exercised on the content of faith as its object—faith alone is the source of the saving knowledge, human reflection on it the instrument of clarification, the means to deepened insight. Instead of treating human thinking in this way, what the gnostics had done, in his view, was to allow human thinking, speculation and imagination, to usurp the place of faith. They allowed it, in his words, 'to alter its subject-matter' (*AH* I.10.3). Here we

have the first and in its simplicity perhaps the classical statement of the Christian theologian's task, which was to remain, substantially, the view of the main current of
subsequent Christian tradition. Theology was seen as putting at the service of faith whatever intellectual equipment
is available and relevant.[1]

We shall have to pass over all the great theologians, who,
as it seems to me, have remained fundamentally faithful to
the view of their work as defined by Irenaeus—Clement of
Alexandria, Origen, Athanasius, the Cappadocian fathers
and the great figures of Latin Christendom. I shall come
straight to the greatest theologian of them all, St. Augustine. His position on this question is basically the same as
that of Irenaeus. If there is a difference between the two,
on this question of faith and human reflection, it is more one
of emphasis and motive than one of substance. Augustine
was not concerned, like Irenaeus, to define the respective
functions of faith and reason in the face of a heretical movement founded precisely on confusing their roles. Augustine's
spiritual pilgrimage had brought him to faith in the incarnate Word. Platonism, as we have noticed repeatedly in
these pages, had been a stage on that journey: it had been
a means of delivering him from his materialist error. It had
been, for him, a true 'preparation for the Gospel', true
especially because it was a preparation and not a substitute.
It was powerless, as he saw after his conversion, to disclose
the saving truth of God's self-revelation in Christ. But faith
once firmly established could only be deepened by having

[1]Cf. my paper 'Pleroma and fulfilment: the significance of
history in St. Irenaeus's opposition to gnosticism' in *Vigiliae
Christianae* 8 (1954), pp. 193–224. Some of the views there expressed should be modified in the light of the paper by R. McL.
Wilson, 'Gnostic origins' in *Vigiliae Christianae*, 9 (1955), pp. 193–
211.

all his mind brought into relation with it. His philosophical equipment always remained for Augustine, part of the means of increasing the depth and the range of his insight into the content of faith. Faith, as we already noted,[1] was the first step along the road to truth, which ended only in the fullness of the truth being disclosed to man in the vision of God. This fullness of understanding is the reward and the goal of faith; but all man's life, in so far as it is rational, spiritual, is a growth in understanding. 'Far be it from us', Augustine writes in one of his letters, 'to suppose that God abhors in us that by virtue of which he has made us superior to other animals. Far be it, I say, that we should believe in order that we may reject reason, or cease to seek it; since we could not even believe unless we possessed rational souls' (*Ep.* 120.3). With him, it is not so much a question of *finding* a place for reason, for reflection, as it had been for Irenaeus; faith *requires* reason and reflection to attain its truly human fullness, for a living faith must be a continual growth of faith in understanding. There is the same insistence here which we noticed in Tertullian on faith as the only way to the saving knowledge of God, on the radical novelty and absolute transcendence of it over against human speculation. But how very far we are from Tertullian's repudiation of human intellectual activity can be gauged from the comparison of Tertullian's remarks on the Gospel texts 'seek and ye shall find, knock and it shall be opened to you'.[2] For Tertullian, as we saw, these promises were valid only on the way to faith: once this is found, there is no further quest. For Augustine, it is only then that the real journey begins: faith has put the believer on the right road, showed the right direction—now, and now alone, is growth in under-

[1]See above, pp. 67–68.
[2]See above, pp. 139–140.

standing possible. And he always interprets these Gospel promises in the sense that it is to faith and faith alone that this growth is vouchsafed.

This is how Augustine comes to formulate the classical type of Christian intellectualism. There is nothing, in the whole field of intellectual disciplines, according to his way of looking at things, that is irrelevant to this quest of understanding in faith. In his treatise *de Doctrina Christiana* he indicates how all the spheres of human inquiry are involved in achieving a better understanding of the Scriptures: in the course of the programme for a Christian culture which he outlines in this work, the sciences of language, history, geography, mathematical and natural sciences, all find their place. Much of this may be a little too naïve in the way in which these intellectual disciplines are seen as related to the understanding of Scripture; and certainly, Augustine's horizon is limited by the fundamentally rhetorical ideal of culture which he shared with his age. But what is vitally important about it is the ideal of a complete human culture consecrated to the service of faith which it is an attempt to embody. This theological humanism is a very distinctively Augustinian ideal. As we shall see, St. Thomas's very much more rigorous discussion of the logic of theological thinking, remained, fundamentally, within this Augustinian perspective.

Hitherto, when speaking of 'philosophy' and of 'theology', we have used the words in their normal, currently accepted sense, to designate two different intellectual disciplines. It would be a mistake to assume that *philosophia* and *theologia* meant much the same to a Greek philosopher or to a Christian Father as they do to us. *Philosophia*, to take this first, always had what one might call a 'totalitarian' sense throughout antiquity, pagan as well as Christian. It suggested the complete whole of human knowledge, about the world, about man and his place in it, at any rate, in so far as this knowedge was significant. *Philosophia* included the treatment of all questions which were a matter of ultimate concern to man: questions about the physical cosmos, about the gods, and about man's place in relation to both: in short, it dealt with everything that was deemed relevant to determining the posture which it was fitting for man to adopt in the world. To have found the right answer to all these questions was wisdom, *sophia*; and the intellectual activity concerned to seek the answers is the quest, or love of wisdom, *philosophia*. Groups of a philosopher's disciples, as early as the Pythagorean school, one of the outstanding examples of this process, tended to form themselves into something very much like religious communities. Often these involved adherence to a definite scheme of life, with rules laid down by or attributed to the founder of the school. The philosophic life was widely held to imply a break with the accepted standards of society, and asceticism, self-denial and the renunciation of worldly goods often formed an important part of its discipline. Through all the various formulations of the ideal life by different philosophical schools runs the notion of deliverance or salvation as the goal. All this made it easy for 'conversion to philosophy' to be thought of in very much the same way as 'conversion to Christianity', or even as binding oneself by monastic vows came later to be thought of.[1]

It was easy, therefore, to represent Christianity as the crown of what was best in antiquity. Notwithstanding the fact that some of the basic beliefs of Christians cut across

[1] On the whole of this paragraph, cf. A. D. Nock, *Conversion: the old and the new in religion from Alexander the Great to Augustine of Hippo* (Oxford, 1933), Ch. 11.

accepted standards of intellectual respectability, in general, its way of life and some of its beliefs were not so radically novel as to find no parallel in paganism. Hence the readiness of Christian writers to follow the established usage in referring to the Christian religion as 'philosophy'. For early Christian writers, too, *philosophia* included the whole of man's attitude to the world and to destiny. Very early in Christian literature we find references to 'Christian philosophy'. Even as 'unphilosophical' a writer as Tatian— 'unphilosophical' in our modern sense—can allow himself to speak of Christianity as a 'philosophy': in speaking of 'our barbarian philosophy' he is concerned to affirm the superiority of Christianity to the error and depravity of paganism, even at its best (*Or.* 35.1). Writers who are at the very opposite pole to Tatian in the value they set upon pagan thought and culture share the same usage. Thus Minucius Felix, the 'Christian Cicero' of the third century, after tracing some of the anticipations of Christianity in pagan thought, concludes in a phrase which echoes Plato (*Rep.* 473D) that 'either Christians are now philosophers, or philosophers had already been Christians' (*Oct.* 20.1).

St. Augustine brings both these attitudes together, still within the same linguistic framework. 'Can paganism,' he asks, 'produce any better philosophy than our Christian, the one true philosophy?' (*c. Julian.* IV. 14.72). Christian 'philosophy', as we have already noted, is, to his mind, wisdom and understanding based on faith. It is because it takes its stand on faith, which starts man's intellectual quest along the right road, that Christian 'philosophy' is superior to any other. Faith, though quite beyond the reach of man's own intellectual effort, is part of *philosophia* thus understood: indeed, it is its beginning, and essential first principle. A faithless 'philosophy' is doomed to error and distortion.

Christian 'philosophy' is a successful attempt to do what all philosophy, pagan and Christian alike, seek to do: 'the only reason man has for philosophizing is that he may attain happiness' (*de Civ. Dei*, XIX. 1.3). Philosophy, in the last resort, is man's quest for beatitude, and includes not only his faith and its expansion into the fullness of understanding but his will and love as well.

If it is impossible to identify the *philosophia* of the Fathers with the intellectual discipline we call 'philosophy', it would be equally untenable to say that it corresponds to what we should call 'theology'. Again, our concept is very much narrower and more definite. The history of the notion of 'theology' would amply repay study; but this raises questions too complicated to pursue here. However it came about, and whatever the consequences, *theologia*— talk about or knowledge of God or gods—had, well before Christian times, entered the field of philosophical disciplines. Philosophical knowledge of the world, it was held by several schools, could lead to or involve knowledge of the divine world. This sort of knowledge was sharply contrasted with the *theologia* involved in religious ritual, mythology and the official state worship, and distinguished from these by the qualifying epithet 'natural' (or 'physical', in the Greek form). It was in this 'natural theology' of paganism, and particularly of the Platonic tradition, that Augustine found some anticipations of the truths taught by Christianity. Here, in his eyes, Greek philosophy had something to offer, which had to be taken seriously, being based on rational insight into the nature of things. The other kinds of pagan 'theology', however, being the product of human fancy and convention, are rejected as being concerned with man-made gods. In salvaging this 'philosophical theology' from the repudiation of pagan religion, Augustine stood within a tradition already established even in some pagan intellectual circles, in which the distinction between 'natural' and 'conventional' gods was by no means unheard of.

For Augustine this distinction was the means that enabled him to treat Neoplatonism, even in what it had to say about divine things, as a preparation of the Gospel. It was not until the Middle Ages that 'natural theology' came to be thought of as a definite intellectual discipline. Its emergence to this status belongs to the story of the second crisis of Christian thought, the upheaval in its structure occasioned by another encounter with antiquity, as a result of its being brought face to face with Aristotelian philosophy in the thirteenth century. Through various sources, various elements of Aristotelian thought had become acclimatized within the tradition of Christian thought. But by and large this tradition had been formed by the unquestioned authority of St. Augustine, and it had, in general, remained loyal to its formative influence. Whatever novelty had found its way into the teaching of the schools, could easily find its place in the Augustinian scheme of faith as the gateway to understanding, and of philosophy as the faith-informed quest of understanding. There was no duality of faith and reason, such as we acknowledge in distinguishing theological from philosophical disciplines. There was still only the one wisdom, which lay in the rational understanding of faith. The movement tending to question this tradition began in the twelfth century, gathered momentum and completely changed the scene by the end of the thirteenth century. As a result of various factors of which by far the most important was the appearance in the West of Latin translations of Aristotle's works, this unitary 'wisdom' was brought face to face with a rival claimant to the title, that of Aristotelian philosophy.

C.F.–L*

Acquaintance with the Aristotelian corpus in itself was enough to tend to disrupt the established tradition of learning. In so far as this tradition was considered as all-of-a-piece, with Platonic conceptual equipment so firmly wedded to the quest of rational insight into Christian faith, a new conceptual scheme inevitably challenged the established tradition. To make the situation even more complicated and delicate, the newly discovered conceptual equipment was often found in the service of intellectual concerns scarcely compatible with preserving the Christian faith in its integrity. The answer to this challenge which gradually established itself was shaped largely by the work of St. Albert the Great and St. Thomas Aquinas. It consisted in an effective and relevant re-assertion of two simple truths: first, that philosophical thinking, like other human disciplines, had its own methods of procedure and was autonomous within its own field. It was not, in other words, to be judged in terms of an established theological tradition, by reference primarily to its value in rendering intelligible the contents of that tradition. We are within sight here of 'philosophy' as a human intellectual discipline conceived in much the same way as we nowadays think of philosophical activity. Coupled with this assertion of the autonomy of philosophy as a rational, human discipline, went the assertion of the freedom of theological thinking to draw upon whatever rational disciplines appeared to have anything to offer that was relevant to and could be utilized in the work of rendering intelligible the divine revelation believed by faith.

To grant philosophy its autonomy and to assert the theologian's freedom to use whatever intellectual structures seem to him to commend themselves, inevitably gave rise to a theology cast in new, Aristotelian, moulds. St. Thomas uses Aristotelian notions in many of his theological analyses. Some of these we have seen at work in his theory of knowledge and mind, of will and love, of virtue, and there are many more and some of more fundamental importance which have fallen outside the scope of the present discussion. One of the most important, because architectonic, concepts he used in the construction of his systematic theology is that of the *scientia*, the Aristotelian *episētmē*. With the aid of this notion he was enabled to give an account of theological thinking as a 'scientific' discipline in the Aristotelian sense.[1] The new conceptual structure and new methods of procedure did not, however, alter the nature of the theologian's business. As in Irenaeus's description of the theologian's task, or Augustine's, or the medieval Augustinians', the goal was still to 'understand what we believe'. The understanding aimed at was to be had fully only in the knowledge of God granted to those who see him face to face: their knowledge is a sharing in the knowledge God has of himself and of his creatures. This knowledge is inaccessible to man, utterly beyond the reach of his natural intellectual capacities. It can only be begun in him through divine initiative, through God revealing himself and man responding to the Word of God in faith. Faith, the God-given adhesion of man to the God of the Bible, is the source and the beginning of all knowledge of God. It is a total subordination of man's mind to God's, involving his whole person and hence his whole intellectual world. God has addressed man in human language; man's response can

---

[1]cp. M.-D. Chenu, *La théologie comme science au XIIIe siècle* (Paris, 1957); also, V. White, 'The theologian's task' in *God the unknown and other essays* (London, 1955), pp. 3–15; and my paper 'Theological thinking—two accounts: Barth and Aquinas' in *Scottish journal of theology*, 10 (1957), pp. 253–61.

only be in the words God has put in his mouth. All his human intellectual activities cannot add to these, or add to them only at the cost of erecting an idol to replace the God of Abraham, Isaac and Jacob. They can only help him to translate the Biblical language into his own, to expound its meaning, to embody its substance in his own language, thought and action. This intellectual expansion of faith in the mind is theology: the theologian's work consists in displaying the believing community's faith by bringing to bear upon it all that is serviceable and relevant in the field of human disciplines. The intellectual obedience of faith thus organized into a total subordination of man's mind to God's is the aim of theological work: 'that it may be an imprint, so to speak, of God's own knowledge', as St. Thomas states it (*S.T.*, 1*a*, 1.3 *ad* 2).

Theology, or *sacra doctrina*, as St. Thomas prefers to call the activity of which we have summarized his account, must be sharply distinguished from the activity we sometimes speak of as 'natural theology'.[1] For Aquinas, as we have seen, faith is the foundation and source of all theological thinking, and God, in his revelation as recorded in the Bible, is its subject-matter. But he does recognize that certain approaches of merely human knowledge may point in some inchoate way towards God. His famous 'five ways' are attempts to focus attention on the world in such a way as to allow us to see it as pointing beyond itself, as merging into mystery at its limits, into a mystery which the world itself compels us to affirm. In this mystery the believer recognizes the God of the Bible in one of his relations to his creation. Such human knowledge pointing towards God is, for

[1] cp. A. R. Motte, 'Théodicée et théologie chez S. Thomas d'Aquin', in *Revue des sciences philosophiques et théologiques*, 26 (1937), pp. 5–26.

Aquinas, generically different from the knowledge given in faith, based on God's own self-disclosure. 'Natural theology', as a consequence, is not theology at all, in the strict sense he gives to *sacra doctrina*. Whatever we may now say about the claims of this kind of thinking, St. Thomas would have thought of it as knowledge about the world more properly than about God. It could aspire to know what he calls the *praeambula* of faith, the anchorage of what we believe by faith in our knowledge of the world. It could never lay claim to knowledge about God in the same sense of 'about' as faith gave knowledge 'about' God, or philosophy 'about' the world.

From St. Justin Martyr onwards—and we might even trace the line back to St. Paul—Christians had represented the best in paganism as an anticipation of the full truth of Christianity. Sometimes, their formulations of this view lay open to the danger of appearing, at least, to compromise the uniqueness and utter transcendence of God's revelation of himself in his Word. This had been the danger of Justin's view. But its great virtue was that it provided a much-needed formula to justify Christian attempts to reach a *modus vivendi* with pagan culture. By Augustine's time the attempt had been made, and in large measure succeeded. Its very success made it even more urgent to reassert what lay behind the repudiation of pagan thought by men like Tatian or Tertullian. Language such as Justin's, which spoke of the seminal *logos* at work in men's minds before, though not fully and wholly disclosed until the coming of the Word to dwell among men, could easily do less than justice to the novelty of revelation. It is one thing to insist with St. Justin, and indeed with the New Testament itself, that even before and outside his revelation God 'did not leave himself without witness' (Acts 14.17); and quite another to pass from this insistence to thinking of a twofold revelation of God, one in his Word, the other in nature. But to speak of the Word as fragmentarily present in nature —unexceptionable as such language is in itself—makes it easy to think of God's self-disclosure in his historical revelation and its consummation in the Incarnation of the Word as no more than the culmination and gathering into one whole of the scattered fragments of an alleged 'natural revelation'. In this way the radical novelty of God's revelation in Jesus Christ is compromised. Christian tradition has always been tempted by the attraction of such a view; at the same time it has always found within itself the resources for a protest against it. Such protests have sometimes gone so far as to belittle the scope and relevance of human intellectual disciplines. St. Thomas's distinction between the generically different activities of exercising reason within the setting of faith and exercising it outside such a setting is an effective safeguard both against succumbing to the temptation to do away with the 'absurdity' of faith, and against the exaggeration of the protest. Although his method of procedure as well as much of the conceptual structure utilized in the course of his work was new, he stood, here as in so many respects, in the main stream of Christian tradition. His analysis of the part reason has to play in the faithful mind expresses the perennial demand made on the Christian theologian: that he should always acknowledge himself as 'debtor both to Greeks and barbarians, both to the wise and to the foolish' (Rom. 1.14); and that he should ceaselessly examine himself in respect of the quality of his indebtedness to the wisdom of men on the one hand, and to the foolishness of the Cross on the other.

INDEX

(Scriptural references are printed in italic)

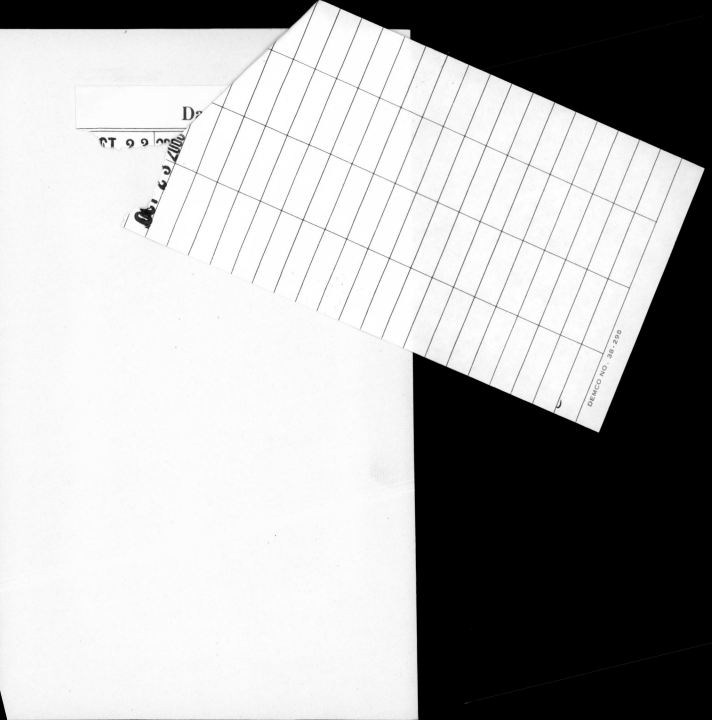

DEMCO NO. 38-298